Mike Forbes & *David Hayward*

British Lorries
Since 1945

Ian Allan
PUBLISHING

ACKNOWLEDGEMENTS

First published 2012

ISBN 978 07110 3647 5

© Mike Forbes and David Hayward 2012

Published by Ian Allan Publishing
An imprint of Ian Allan Publishing Ltd, Hersham, Surrey KT12 4RG
Printed in England by Ian Allan Printing Ltd, Hersham, Surrey KT12 4RG

Visit the Ian Allan website at www.ianallanpublishing.com

On the eve of this book going to press, I was shocked and saddened by the news that **David Hayward**, my co-author, had died suddenly. Without his invaluable input, the book would not be nearly as comprehensive. It stands as a tribute to David's work and is therefore dedicated to his memory.

Mike Forbes

The authors wish to thank the following for their assistance:

Stewart Bebbington, John Byrne, Geoff Carverhill, Keith Child, Sandy Glen, Andrew Grant, David Hambleton, Chris Hodge, Doug Jack, Roy Larkin, Ian Maclean, Phil Moth, David Riley, Chris Taylor, Graeme Turner and Tim West.

Photographs have been taken from the Ian Allan Library and their original copyright holders are acknowledged where known. Others have been supplied by Phil Moth of PM Photography and the Chris Hodge Commercials (CHC) Stilltime collection. (Numbers are quoted for the latter.)

Previous page Seen parked together, these three 1965 ERF KV-cabbed four-wheelers were from the fleet of Showerings of Shepton Mallet, manufacturers of Babycham. Some operators opted to continue to use the 'Kleer-Vue' cab, although it had been superseded by the LV. *PM Photography*

CONTENTS

INTRODUCTION

Our society has become increasingly reliant upon the lorry in all its different forms, for everything from our daily bread to the movement of industrial goods in and out of the country. It is, in fact, an essential part of everybody's life. Note that we use the term 'lorry' rather than the modern 'truck', as it seems more appropriate for the majority of vehicles discussed here. In military parlance, a 'truck' was a vehicle weighing up to 1 ton and a 'lorry' was above that weight.

Previously, long-distance transport had been the province of the railways or coastal shipping, but our roads and the vehicles which use them have developed to such an extent over the last 100 years that other modes of transport are unable to compete – in terms of convenience, productivity and, above all, price. Our road network may be far from perfect, but these days lorries can reach almost anywhere in the British Isles safely and quickly, carrying the heaviest or bulkiest of loads.

Today there are also large numbers of road-transport enthusiasts who enjoy watching present-day vehicles and following the fortunes of their favourite fleets. Many are interested in older vehicles, attending rallies, buying models, photographs, magazines or books devoted to their favourite subject. And here, of course, is another one…

This is a thorough update of a volume which has been published several times before by Ian Allan in different forms. This time we are concentrating on the period from the end of World War 2 up to the present day, which we believe will be of most interest to the majority of readers. During this period the lorry has evolved from a rather basic vehicle, of which the driver could almost count himself lucky if it possessed a roof and a seat. In many cases he would literally wrestle his vehicle along the road with its underpowered engine, without the aid of power steering or synchromesh gearbox, enduring cold in winter and heat in summer with no thought for his comfort or well-being. The driver usually had to manhandle his load of heavy bags or crates on and off the vehicle, as well as sheeting and roping before setting off. Long-distance transport would usually entail 'nights out', sometimes in poorly-appointed accommodation.

These days, drivers work in comparative luxury in a comfortable cab, usually air-conditioned, hauling unit loads in a vehicle where just about everything is power-assisted and mechanical handling equipment makes short work of loading or unloading at each end of the journey. On the other hand, they usually have to spend their nights away from home in the sleeper cab, with fewer roadside facilities – good or bad – available for a meal, rest or recuperation.

There have been many technical advances: the almost complete move to diesel power; tilt-cabs to ease maintenance – although better oils and other improvements mean less frequent servicing; the increasing use and perfection of hydraulics – not just for tippers but for everything from power steering to swap-bodies; articulation has almost completely replaced multi-wheeled rigids and draw-bar trailers for maximum weight vehicles (apart from some specialised applications); curtain-siders have replaced sheeting and roping loads on flats, while advances in refrigeration and insulation have meant that temperature-controlled vehicles are available for many perishable goods.

At the start of the period covered by this book, the driver would also have been expected to carry out his own repairs and certainly to change a wheel at the side of the road – usually with the assistance of other drivers, who would not think of passing another lorry driver who had broken down. These days, apart from the Health & Safety aspect of working on a vehicle at the side of the road, it would probably not be possible to repair many of a vehicle's faults, as its mechanics are largely controlled by computer.

This book charts such developments over the last 65 years or so, mainly using contemporary pictures of lorries at work, often when new, taken for the commercial vehicle magazines of the time. We have tried to represent each successive type and style of vehicle from every company which manufactured lorries in the British Isles over the years – although we have excluded some, for example export-only and 'rebuilding' companies, while car-derived vans and most light commercials would be better covered in a separate volume of their own.

A lot of names in this book may be unfamiliar to the younger reader, who might only have seen them at a preserved vehicle rally. Indeed, changes in the motor vehicle industry have meant that most of these manufacturers are now very much relegated to history.

Without delving into the economic or political backgrounds to this, it is sufficient to say that motor-vehicle manufacture has become far more international in nature over the last 30 to 40 years. Economies of scale dictate that the same sort of vehicle is used in many different countries. Only where there are particular circumstances - such as very hot or cold climates, or a total lack of conventional roads - are special vehicles called upon these days.

This was certainly not the case some years back, when there was a definite preference by most operators to use vehicles made in this country. The British Isles were once considered to be the workshop of the world, never truer than with regard to motor vehicles. However, the UK seems to have lost its way in this respect. Whether management, unions or other factors are to blame, nearly all indigenous manufacturers have now been taken over or closed. Foreign-built lorries make up nearly all the fleets you will see on the road in the UK.

Continental lorries have their fans, of course, but the traditional British products are the ones we all remember with affection - even if they broke down, making ever harder work of the driver's life. The range of different manufacturers was surprisingly wide, some of which were quite small companies which made vehicles for a few years before fading into obscurity. We remember them all in these pages and encourage the reader to seek out these unusual names which are part of our transport and industrial heritage.

Similarly, the operators have changed, with the takeover of smaller fleets by larger combines, which themselves have more recently become parts of international conglomerates. It is interesting to look back at what were once well-known names, either nationally or locally. The mix of own-account operators (which move their own goods) and transport contractors has changed, with ever more vehicles on contract hire, usually with the customer's livery obscuring the actual operator's identity.

There have been many other outside influences on the transport industry over the years. Firstly, vehicles changed with the move to bulk handling of some loads and the containerisation of many others. Secondly, political changes first resulted in the nationalisation of much of the industry, when British Road Services was created in the late 1940s, and then partial denationalisation during the early 1950s. (Depending on how they fared during the upheaval, the BRS set-up is held in high esteem by some transport people and hated by others.) In Ireland, Córas Iompair Éireann (CIÉ) was founded and moved into road transport, this too being nationalised in 1950.

Operators'/drivers' licensing and hours have also changed, particularly due to the UK Transport Act 1968 but also as a result of adopting European Union legislation. Above all, there have been regular changes to the Construction & Use regulations, notably allowing heavier weights and dimensions for goods vehicles, partly to keep up with changing international standards and partly thanks to improved roads and vehicle technology.

All of these changes and developments will become apparent as you read through this book, as well as the manufacturers' and operators' responses. It makes it all the more fascinating to follow the fortunes of the transport industry during the period in question and to study the different vehicles.

ABBREVIATIONS

Throughout this book, a number of accepted transport-industry abbreviations are used:

ulw   unladen weight
gvw   gross vehicle weight
gtw   gross train weight (usually including a trailer)
gcw   gross combination weight (applied to articulated vehicles)
TIR   Transports Internationaux Routiers or International Road Transports – a 1975 convention on international transport under TIR carnets, to simplify and speed movement of goods in sealed containers through customs, without repeated border checks.
cwt   hundredweight (20 to the ton)
kg   kilogram (1,000kg = one tonne*)

lhd   left-hand drive
lwb   long wheelbase
rhd   right-hand drive
swb   short wheelbase
hp   horsepower
bhp   brake horsepower
GRP   glass fibre-reinforced plastic
PSV   public-service vehicle
ft   feet
cu m   cubic metres
cu yd   cubic yards

Tonnes is the metric measure used in more recent years, slightly less than the old imperial ton used in respect of older vehicles.

AEC

The Associated Equipment Co (AEC) was set up to build London's buses in 1906. The works was moved from Walthamstow to Southall, Middlesex, in 1927, and remained there until the end. From the 1930s, AEC used names beginning with 'M' for its goods vehicles – including Mercury, Majestic, Mammoth, Mammoth Major and Mandator – and continued using some of these post-war.

During World War 2 the company switched to war production, building thousands of military vehicles including the four-wheel-drive Matador. In 1948, the company restarted civilian production with the four-wheeled 12-ton gvw Monarch and Matador, which could also be used to tow a trailer, the six-wheeled 19-ton gvw Mammoth Major 6 and the eight-wheeled 22-ton gvw Mammoth Major 8.

After the acquisition in 1948 of the Maudslay Motors Co Ltd of Alcester, near Coventry (see page 135), and the long-established Manchester-based Crossley Motors Ltd, AEC became a holding company known as Associated Commercial Vehicles (ACV) Ltd, though all AEC lorries and passenger-carrying chassis retained AEC badging. Subsequently, in 1949, ACV acquired coachbuilders Park Royal Vehicles (PRV) of West London and its subsidiary Charles H. Roe of Leeds. In 1953 a new 8-ton Mercury was launched, with a PRV-designed cab fitted later. (PRV subsequently supplied cabs for other AEC models.)

Along with other rival companies, AEC moved into the market for civil-engineering construction vehicles. In 1957, the company offered a large six-wheeled 10 cu yd Dumptruk, which was followed by other variants – up to and including an 18 cu yd four-axle version – until production ended in 1967.

Subsequently, Transport Equipment (Thornycroft) Ltd of Basingstoke, Hampshire (see page 172) was also taken over. Production of the Thornycroft range continued, but it concentrated on firefighting vehicles and heavy tractor units.

In August 1962, ACV merged with Leyland Motors Ltd (see page 113), after which AEC – just like Thornycroft, Albion and Scammell – began to lose its independent identity. In 1964, the Leyland-designed Ergomatic cab (made by Joseph Sankey of Birmingham – later GKN Sankey and also used by Albion, as well as Leyland) was adopted alongside PRV-built cabs. However, Leyland Motors' management subsequently ordered a rationalisation of the range, particularly after the merger in 1968 with British Motor Holdings which created the British Leyland Motor Corporation Ltd (BLMC).

From 1973, Southall started building Leyland-badged vehicles – including the Marathon, designed in-house – as well as AECs until 1977, when the AEC name was dropped completely on commercial chassis in favour of 'Leyland'. By April 1979, when the works closed for good, the company was still building AEC-badged public-service vehicles as well as the Leyland Marathon 2 from 1977, before its production moved to Scammell in Watford (see page 149). The site was used as a storage facility for London buses for a time, before demolition and redevelopment.

Right: This AEC Monarch, registered in London in 1948, was employed with various other tippers, including pre-war AECs, by sand and gravel company Hall & Co during the 1950s, at what is believed to have been near the site of London (Heathrow) Airport. It has a typical cab for its era, to a style used by a number of coachbuilders.
Chris Hodge Commercial aau745

Left: A 1954 Mammoth Major 8 Mk III with 11.3-litre engine, fitted with a triple-deck SMT (Scottish Motor Traction) body in service with W. Speak of Llanbyther, Carmarthenshire. It was used to transport sheep, lambs or dairy cows. *ACV Sales Ltd*

Left: The AEC works was located in Windmill Lane, Southall, Middlesex, from whence the local council understandably ordered its own fleet. This Mercury with Park Royal 'tin front' cab was new in March 1955, with a 10¼ cu yd Edbro tipping body and canvas cover. The new cab design was by then available alongside the more-traditional 'vertical radiator' type. *ACV Sales Ltd*

Left: AEC produced a series of heavy six-wheel tippers under the Dumptruk name, with various different cabs and bodies. This is an early example from 1956, built for the Ministry of Supply, which has an Edbro 24½-ton/10 cu yd body. From about 1964, Scammell built similar vehicles under the AEC, Scammell and Aveling Barford names. *ACV Sales Ltd*

Right: State-owned British Road Services Ltd was a major AEC customer for many years. This 1958-registered 'tin-front' Mandator tractor unit, fleet No 1A362, is seen coupled to a 33ft platform trailer. It was allocated to the Hampstead, North-West London branch. *Ian Allan Library*

Right: Photographed in 1962, this 1961-registered Mandator Mk V tractor, 415 BGO, was in service with Shell-Mex and BP Ltd. It was fitted with the AV690 engine and coupled to a 3700-gallon, two-compartment tank body on a Carrimore trailer. Note the front-mounted silencer, in order to comply with the Petroleum Regulations. *ACV Sales Ltd*

Right: This eight-wheeled, 1963-registered Mammoth Major Mk V was No 1 in the fleet of Heavy Haulage Specialists of Waltham Cross, Hertfordshire. Note the use of the two-axle 'dolly' to carry the long load. *AEC Ltd*

Left: This 1964 Mercury tractor, BRS no RA263, was photographed in June 1966. It is seen here coupled to a single-axle platform trailer, being loaded with prefabricated houses by a mobile crane. *BRS*

Left: After the merger with Leyland Motors, AEC shared the new Sankey 'Ergomatic' cab with Leyland and Albion lorries. No D1 was London Brick Company Ltd's first 16-ton gvw Mercury with the AV505 engine, six-speed overdrive gearbox and modern (at the time) power-assisted steering. *AEC*

Above: ICI Dyestuffs Division No N24 was a 1966 six-wheeled, twin-steer, 'Ergomatic'-cabbed Mammoth Minor tractor. It was rated at 32 tons gtw on five axles and was carrying polymer chips on a two-axle trailer in Impalco aluminium Tote bins. This was the raw material for Bri-nylon which was delivered from ICI's Wilton works to ICI Fibres Ltd factories. *AEC*

Below: AEC bonneted lorries proved particularly popular with the export market. This Mogul, fitted with a locally built cab, was in service with a Rotterdam haulier on TIR work throughout Europe, including the UK. *Ian Allan Library*

Left: This 1967 National Coal Board 6x4 Marshall is fitted with a 24ft long coal-tanker body with a 23.5 cu yd capacity, built by Atkinson's of Clitheroe. *Ian Allan Library*

Below: This 1969 Mercury 4x2 chassis, with tipper body and Hiab loader, appears to be brand new. It had the AV505 151bhp engine and was rated at 16 tons gvw. *AEC*

Above: R. Sinclair Junior, a transport contractor based in Evesham, operated this summer 1969-registered Mandator tractor. The 32-ton gvw tractor had the AEC 800 (247bhp) or 801 (272bhp) V8 engine and a six- or 10-speed semi-automatic transmission. *AEC*

Right: London Brick's 1973-registered Marshall six-wheeler, with a York 'Selfstak' body. It is seen being loaded with a brick container by a Freightliner gantry at a company rail-connected depot. *Ian Allan Library*

Right: This 30-ton gvw Mammoth Major 8 tipper with AV760 engine was registered in late 1972. It was used by a Parkstone, Dorset-based sand and ballast merchant, E. F. Phillips & Sons Ltd. *Ian Allan Library*

Below: The style of grille seen on this Mammoth Major fuel tanker in the Wincanton Transport fleet was used on most AECs during the 1970s. The 'Ergo' cab was not raised, however, as on later Leylands. *PM Photography*

ALBION

The Albion Motor Car Co Ltd was formed at Scotstoun, near Glasgow, in 1901. In 1931, the word 'car' was dropped from the company name; in 1935, Albion took over Halley Motors Ltd (founded 1906) of Yoker, not far from the Scotstoun works.

During World War 2, Albion built military lorries, including 3-ton 4x4 and 10-ton 6x4 tractors for tank transporters. Civilian model production recommenced in 1947, with a range of six chassis: the 14-ton 8x4 payload CX7, 12-ton 6x4 CX5, 7-ton CX1, 6-ton 4x2 CX3, 4/5-ton FT3 and 1-ton AZ5. Improved versions of these and other new models followed at intervals over the next few years. However, in 1951 the company was acquired by Leyland Motors Ltd and, although production continued, the Leyland influence gradually made itself felt. The company also restarted military lorry production again.

In 1955, Albion introduced the 3 and 4 ton respectively Model MR5 and MR7 Claymore chassis, which had an underfloor Leyland 0.300 diesel engine. The 1954-7 MLH3 Cairn was a 30-35-cwt version, with lighter axles. The cab was mounted forward of the front axle, which afforded a good turning circle with the maximum body length for the size of the vehicle, ideal for local delivery and collection work. The 16-ton payload Caledonian 8x4 was introduced in 1958 as a general competitor to the Leyland Octopus (sharing the same cab, in fact). By then, the 1958-65 3-5 ton respectively CL5/CL7 Claymore with Austin axles replaced the Albion/axled MR5/MR7.

From then on, Albion shared the same basic cab designs, including the LAD cab shared with Dodge and the Ergomatic design with AEC and Leylands.

In 1968, Leyland Motors merged with the BMC to form the British Leyland Motor Corporation Ltd. Production continued with the Albion Chieftain, Clydesdale and Reiver lorries and the Albion Viking bus chassis. In 1969, the company took over the neighbouring Coventry Ordnance Works on South Street, from which it continues to operate.

By 1972, after BMC trucks had been rebadged as 'Leylands', the Albion name was also dropped in favour of 'Leyland' and the company name changed to 'Leyland (Glasgow)'. Lorries and buses continued to be built in Scotstoun, including many smaller Leyland vehicles (notably the Redline range). The plant then stopped building complete vehicles and production moved to Bathgate, West Lothian in 1980; the Albion plant continued but only produced automotive components, including axles.

The company then changed its trading name to 'Leyland DAF' in 1987, when the Leyland Trucks division of the British Rover Group (as it then was) merged with the Dutch DAF Trucks company. The new company, DAF NV, was jointly owned by DAF Beheer BV (60%) and Rover Group (40%).

A management buy-out in 1993 brought Albion Automotive, as it was thenceforth known, back into Scottish ownership for a time. However, new owner, the American Axle & Manufacturing Co (AAM) of Detroit, Michigan, took over Albion in 1998. Today it manufactures axles, driveline systems, chassis systems, crankshafts and chassis components.

Left: This Albion, No 280 on the fleet of Young's Express Deliveries Ltd, was registered in Paisley immediately post-World War 2, and this shot is dated June 1946. It was a petrol-engined FT.3L and rated at 5 tons 2-cwt, with a ulw of 2 tons 18-cwt 2qrt 10lb. *Albion Motors Ltd*

Left: Although not registered, this view of a four-wheeled FT35L Clansman rigid dates from late 1947. The radiator badge indicates it has an Albion oil (diesel) engine. *Albion Motors Ltd*

Left: Although registered in 1951 (the year that Albion Motors merged with Leyland Motors), this FT37 Chieftain four-wheeler was apparently photographed in July 1957. As can be seen, no 140 in the Calor Gas fleet was used to deliver bottled 'town gas' – coal gas for use in houses in rural districts. *Ian Allan Library*

Left: This 1955 4-ton MR7N Claymore delivery lorry had an underfloor Albion EN219 diesel engine, a horizontal four-cylinder unit that shared a design and components with the six-cylinder Leyland O.350. It was in use as a demonstrator with the manufacturer's London sales office, based at their Willesden depot, and was photographed on the North Circular Road on test for Modern Transport magazine. *Ian Allan Library*

Right: Albion Motors adopted the 'long-door' version of the LAD cab it shared with Leyland Motors and Dodge Bros. This model CH3 Chieftain was new in 1960 (although the shot is dated November 1961), was in service with Allen & Day Ltd and had a 950 cu ft insulated container on an aluminium alloy platform, supplied by Federated Industries Ltd of Aberdeen. Up to 1,200 stone (7,620kg) of wet fish could be conveyed from Aberdeen to other ports for export. *Ian Allan Library*

Below: This British Rail model CD21ATR Clydesdale tractor is seen coupled to a BTC/Charrold semitrailer for bulk coal collection and delivery. It was rated at 12 tons and photographed in March 1962. *BR*

Below: Worcester-based John Williams (Cinetic Sand) Ltd had a fleet of Leyland Group vehicles, including this 1965-registered model CH13AT Chieftain Super Six tipper with a 6 cu yd fixed-sided alloy body and Edbro underbody tipping gear. It is seen here being loaded with foundry sand. *Ian Allan Library*

Left: Albion Motors adopted the 'Ergomatic' cab for some models, as seen with this 1966-registered CD65 Super Clydesdale four-wheeler in service with the Scottish subsidiary (based in Govan, Glasgow) of J. Bibby & Sons of Liverpool. This vehicle was used for bulk feed delivery and had a ulw of 6 tons 2-cwt. *Ian Allan Library*

Above: A 1966 Super Reiver model RE33T20 six-wheeled Leyland-engined tipper, No 29 in the fleet of Bradford coal distributor Smith, Parkinson & Cole Ltd. The body was built by Reliance Garage Co (Brighouse) Ltd and had Milshaw TM3R tipping gear. *Ian Allan Library*

Above: This model RE33T Super Reiver 20 six-wheeled tipper photographed new in June 1967, destined for the fleet of Castlehill Sand & Gravel. *Ian Allan Library*

ARGYLE

1970-73

The Argyle Motor Manufacturing Co Ltd was located at College Milton in East Kilbride, Lanarkshire. It was incorporated in early 1970 by Argyle Diesel Electronics Ltd with the intention of assembling lorry chassis to special order in the 16-ton gvw range. The only model offered by 1971 was the Christina, of which production was expected to reach 51 during the year.

The company assembled its own chassis in two wheelbase lengths, including a tipper version, and bought-in proprietary units such as Perkins 6.354 engines and cabs from Motor Panels. The company exhibited at the 1971 Scottish Motor Show and the prototype was apparently tested by Commercial Motor magazine. However, only a few were built.

Below: This Argyle Christina four-wheeled rigid chassis-cab was on display at the 1971 Scottish Motor Show in Kelvin Hall, Glasgow. Note the Motor Panels cab with removable grille for access to the radiator and the front of the Perkins engine. *CHC abk313*

ATKINSON

1933-81

Atkinson Lorries Ltd was founded in 1933, at Walton-le-Dale near Preston, Lancashire, replacing steam-wagon manufacturer Atkinson & Co of Frenchwood, Preston, which dated back to 1907. The new company produced Gardner-engined diesel vehicles from the start, although, when Gardners were unavailable during World War 2, Atkinson continued limited production with AEC engines instead. The famous 'A' in a circle emblem first appeared on the radiator grille in 1937.

After the war the company relaunched its range of four, six and eight-wheeled vehicles, the design of which remained basically unaltered until 1953, when the cabs were redesigned with the familiar bow front. The nationalised British Road Services acquired Atkinson eight-wheeled rigid lorries alongside its other makes.

In 1957, heavier vehicles were marketed with an eye to cross-country and oil-field operations, with the Omega bonneted 100-ton 6x6 vehicles with Rolls-Royce engines bing produced. In 1958, a GRP cab incorporating a wraparound windscreen was made available across most of the range.

During the early 1960s Atkinson began manufacturing the Black Knight range of four, six and eight-wheeled vehicles, Gold Knight chassis for tippers and (swb) concrete mixers, and Silver Knight tractor units. For a time some vehicles were produced with a decorative grille panel, but the exposed radiator held sway. It was even fitted to a few Atkinson vehicles which sported a German Krupp-manufactured cab on a Silver Knight chassis during 1968, with an eye to the European market. In 1966, the Viewline cab was introduced, but it was not very popular with operators and was dropped a few years later.

This Mk I range (as it would be retrospectively known) was then replaced in 1968 by the Borderer 4x2 tractor unit, the Searcher rigid-six and the Defender rigid-eight, with an updated GRP cab complete with a dummy radiator, plus the Omega bonneted 100-ton heavy tractor. The Leader rear-steering tractor unit was launched along with an 8x4 tipper chassis using Gardner 150 or 180 engines, which were also fitted to many of the larger trucks. During the early 1970s, the Searcher 6x4 chassis proved popular for cement mixers. The emphasis, however, was on tractor units, both the Venturer 6x4 and the Borderer 4x2 chassis being offered with a choice of engines (although engines by Gardner or Cummins were usually fitted).

In 1970, after protracted negotiations, Atkinson Lorries Ltd was finally aquired by Seddon Diesel Vehicles Ltd, to form Seddon Atkinson Vehicles

Left: Although registered in Liverpool during World War 2, this Atkinson tractor unit was very similar to the early post-war models (apart from possessing an AEC 7.7-litre engine, rather than a Gardner). It was photographed in this nostalgic scene c1960, being loaded with wool bales from a warehouse. *CHC abe379*

Ltd, but production of the two separate ranges continued. Seddon Atkinson was then taken over in 1974 by the US-owned International Harvester, which also had a European interest via a holding in the Dutch DAF concern. The last 'true' Atkinson, a Defender eight-wheel rigid, was built at the Walton-le-Dale works in 1975.

Alongside Seddon's facility at Oldham, the Atkinson works then assembled the new Seddon Atkinson 400 Series. The range included 12 models: six tractors, rated at 30 or 32 tons gcw, with Gardner, Rolls-Royce or Cummins engines; 30-ton and 32-ton gtw four-wheelers capable of towing a trailer, 24-ton gvw rigid-sixes and 30-ton rigid-eights, with Gardner or Cummins engines for all the last three types. Sleeper cabs could be provided on all chassis. There was also the 200 Series of 16-ton rigid four-wheelers with a choice of three wheelbase lengths, all fitted with International engines. The Atkinson works went on to produce the first batch of the 400 Series' replacement, the 401, but closed in 1981. (For the corresponding history, see page 157, Seddon, and page 162, Seddon Atkinson)

Left: James Arnott & Sons Ltd of Newcastle upon Tyne operated this 1956-registered 4-ton ulw Atkinson L.633. It had a bow-fronted cab, Gardner 4LW engine and 20ft alloy body. Used for delivering engine oil for ships, and carried 8-10 tons of lubricating oils outward and raw materials on the return, making at least a thousand-mile round-trip each week. *Ian Allan Library*

Left: This eight-wheeled L.1786 model produced by Cyprien-Fox Transport Ltd was new in February 1958, equipped with a dropside body and cab-roof sheet-rack to store unused tarpaulins. It was used on long-distance trunk work between London, Manchester, Middlesbrough and Newport. *Ian Allan Library*

Above: The Omega 100-ton 6x6 heavy tractor was introduced in 1957. Although rejected by the British Army, it was exported overseas. This shot dates from March 1960 and shows two units apparently destined for the Middle East: the left is an RV30 and that on the right an RV48 with torque-converter transmission, also fitted with heavy-duty air filtration. The engine used was a 333bhp supercharged six-cylinder Rolls Royce C6.SFL. *Atkinson Vehicles Ltd*

Above: This tractor unit was new in early 1963. It was coupled to a low-loader trailer, conveying a Ruston Thermax boiler from the famous works of Ruston & Hornsby Ltd of Lincoln, and was operated by local haulier DMT Transport Ltd. Unusually, it also had a Ruston air-cooled diesel engine. Note the new-style cab with decorative panel and twin headlamps; this was only used for a short time, as operators preferred the exposed radiator. *Ian Allan Library*

Left: This Cummins-engined tractor was fitted with an unusual 'Clearview' cab. It was numbered U770 in the fleet of famous operator Bulwark Transport Ltd of Chippenham, Wiltshire, and was on the Atkinson stand at the 1964 Earls Court Commercial Motor Show. *CHC aaa083*

Above and right: This six-wheeled heavy-haulage tractor was new in 1966 to Graham Adams of New Malden, Surrey. It was fitted with a 270hp Cummins engine, Allison semi-automatic gearbox and an interesting steel cab, based on one designed for an Atkinson dump truck, complete with 'dog's window'. *CHC abj079/080*

Above: This new Silver Knight tractor unit was No 97 with C. Butt Ltd of Northampton in 1967. It had a Cummins engine and was coupled to a York 'trombone' extending trailer, loaded with pre-cast concrete beams. It was also fitted with the standard Atkinson glass fibre-panelled cab of the day, with dual headlamps. *York Trailers*

Below: It is believed that this August 1967 shot was taken at Atkinson Vehicles Ltd's service centre. On the left is a new Cummins-engined Silver Knight six-wheeled tractor, fitted with the unusual high-screen Viewline cab. On the right is a Cummins-engined tractor from the Pickfords fleet, new in spring 1966, with the earlier style of cab retrospectively referred to as the Mk I. *Ian Allan Library*

Right: This Atkinson Defender eight-wheeler was fitted with a bulk powder tanker body and was part of the large fleet of R. Hanson & Son Ltd of Chapel-en-le-Frith.
PM Photography

Right: W. & J. Riding Ltd was a well-known Atkinson user for many years, as shown by the earlier Borderer in the background of this May 1981 shot. Seddon Atkinson Vehicles Ltd was formed in mid-1970, and the last 'true' Atkinson assembled at Walton-le-Dale in 1975. However, the Atkinson works assembled the Seddon Atkinson 400 Series, and also the first batch of the new 401 model, before closing at the end of 1981. This Atkinson-badged Seddon-Atkinson 400 has a 220bhp turbocharged Gardner 6LXCT engine and is coupled to a bulk powder tanker trailer.
Ian Allan Library

Left: Bassetts of Tittensor had a number of Atkinson Borderer tractor units in its mixed fleet. The Borderer had an up-dated version of the traditional cab, with glass-fibre panels on a wooden frame – even the radiator surround was glass-fibre.
PM Photography

AUSTIN

1905-68

Austin Motor Co Ltd of Longbridge, Birmingham was traditionally a manufacturer of passenger cars and light commercials until 1938, when a new range of 30-cwt to 5-ton lorries was added. During World War 2 Longbridge assembled a range of K Series 4x2 and 4x4 lorries, including the K2, K4, K5 and K32/K39, plus the K6 6x4 chassis.

Post-war, the company continued with its civilian K2 and K4 (Series I) three and five-tonners, until these were updated with a new front-end design in 1950 as the Series II Loadstar models. These were joined by the 25-cwt K8, which was initially offered as the 'Three-way' van – then as a chassis, chassis-cab, ambulance and minibus. All of these continued in production until September 1954.

In 1952, Austin Motor Co Ltd and the Nuffield Group (including Morris Commercial Cars Ltd) merged to form the British Motor Corporation (BMC), which began some unification of the two ranges. By 1956, Longbridge had taken over all chassis assembly over 1½ tons. Identical lorries and vans could now be seen with either Austin or Morris-Commercial (or Morris, as of 1955/6) badging or, in the case of the seven-tonners, the BMC emblem – until 1962, when production moved

to the new Bathgate, West Lothian plant. These vehicles included the Austin version of the Adderley Park-built Morris-Commercial LC4/5 normal control 30-cwt lorry, both of which were replaced in 1960 by the FG. In 1962, FG production moved to Bathgate as well.

In addition to commercial models, Austin continued with post-war military production. The K9 4x4 was introduced in 1952, derived from the civilian Loadstar range but modified to make it more suitable for military service – with a wider track, increased ground clearance and all-wheel drive. Designated the FV16000 Series, it was rated at a very conservative 1 ton and its chassis adapted for use as a cargo vehicle, ambulance or water tanker, with the wireless body being the most numerous variation. It was also available commercially between 1953 and 1955, when it was rated at 1½ tons.

Below: This is an official 1939 shot of a Longbridge-built Austin K2 2-ton long-wheelbase version, with a 3.5-litre straight six petrol engine and dropside body. The radiator grille was modified for post-war vehicles, otherwise there were few changes. Retrospectively, this design became known as the Series I. *Ian Allan Library*

Left: This Austin K2 express parcels van, with the post-war revised grille, was registered in early 1947 and became No m13463 with Carter Paterson and Pickfords Joint Parcels Services. The original engine was replaced by a 4-litre unit in 1948. This type of Austin became known by the nickname 'Birmingham Bedford' because of the similarity of the front-end design to that of contemporary Bedfords. *Ian Allan Library*

Left: In 1950, Longbridge launched the revised Series II with a newly styled cab as the Austin Loadstar. This 1952-registered K2 Luton van was photographed (probably in London) in service with the Ministry of Food's Food Flying Squad – originally a wartime measure but continuing into the 1950s. *Ian Allan Library*

Left: This 1955 tractor unit, with a Scammell fifth wheel, was rated at 5 tons. The engine options were a 68bhp petrol or Perkins P6 diesel. The official ulw was 2 tons 6-cwt 3qrt. This one is seen with a refrigerated van trailer, in service with the Liverpool dairy J. Hanson & Sons Ltd. *Ian Allan Library*

Right: The K9 was introduced in 1952, based on the Loadstar range with a four-litre petrol engine but with additional four-wheel drive, increased track, military tyres and increased ground clearance. The FV16000 Series had a 1-ton military rating and was bodied as ambulances, water tankers and wireless vans. A 1½-ton commercial version was available between 1952 and 1953. In 1955, the 1-ton Series III was launched with a revised BMC normal control cab and four-litre engine, though later production models were powered by a BMC multi-fuel engine. *Ian Allan Library*

Right: The Morris-Commercial FV was introduced in 1948, becoming first Series I and then Series II in 1954/5. The revised cab was badged as an Austin as well as a Morris, after the formation of the British Motor Corporation. This October 1955 shot is of a 3-ton van from the R. J. Bates & Co (London) Ltd fleet. (There was also a 5-ton chassis version.) From 1955, the FE (Series III) used a revised corporate cab and a BMC-badged seven-tonner was added, joining lighter Austin and Morris versions sold by the respective dealers (though both sold BMC-badged lorries). *Ian Allan Library*

Right: This 5-ton Austin FF (Austin 45) was photographed in March 1958. Note the 'BMC' above the 'Austin' badge. In 1958, the Austin/Morris FF replaced the upper end of the FE (Series III) range and was offered in 5, 7 and 8-ton variations – the latter with BMC badges. They were replaced by the similar-looking FH/Austin 45 with a flat cab floor, in 1961. *Ian Allan Library*

Left: The BMC WE with Fisher & Ludlow cab was developed from the Loadstar. This 1958/9 BMC diesel-engined Austin-badged 5-ton tractor with Scammell coupling was used in connection with the newly introduced British Railways London Midland Region 'Condor' express freight service between Manchester and London. *BR*

Left: The Austin and Morris-badged FG was introduced in 1960, with capacities from 1½ to 5 tons, replacing both the normal control LC Series and the lighter end of the forward control FE range. The FG range was rebadged as 'BMC' in 1968. This 1960-registered Fyffes Bananas FG has a curtain-side body. The 1961-68 FM had a modified FG cab with a 'snout' added to allow the engine to be moved further forward, allowing for an extra passenger seat. Production moved to Bathgate in 1962. *Ian Allan Library*

Left: The 1964-8 Bathgate-built Austin and Morris-badged FJ replaced the FH Series. Featuring a new tilt cab, it was available in non-HGV ratings of 5 tons and 7 tons, as the K100 and K140 respectively. Heavier versions were also available, including the 8-ton K160 and 10-ton K360 Prime Mover. This 1968-registered FJ just pre-dated the short-lived BMC badging and was fitted with a tank for authorised Shell-Mex and BP central heating oil distributor Kenning Fuel Supplies of Leicester. *Ian Allan Library*

BEDFORD

Vauxhall Motors Ltd of Luton, Bedfordshire, was acquired by the General Motors Corporation of the USA in 1925. A new line of Chevrolet-based Bedford two-tonners was launched alongside its passenger car range in April 1931, followed a year later, after the Chevrolet name was dropped, by 30-cwt commercial chassis and subsequently by dedicated PSV chassis, as well as 12-cwt light vans.

The company produced around 249,000 military lorries during World War 2, as well as civilian versions of utilitarian military designs, and in 1940 militarised civilian lorries. The company reverted to civilian production again in 1947, with designs introduced immediately pre-war. The K, M and O Series competed, in many cases, with auctioned-off former military vehicles, although large numbers of refurbished wartime models were also utilised by the forces for many years post-war.

In 1950, the first of the 'Big Bedfords' was launched, the S Type semi-forward control, with a new cab and a range of wheelbases, as both a seven-tonner and swb 10-ton tractor unit with Scammell automatic coupling. The pre-war style bonneted types were replaced by the new TA Series normal control design with a brand new US-style cab in 1953, including an 8-ton tractor unit, again with Scammell coupling.

In 1952, Vauxhall then introduced a new 4x4 version of the S Type, the R Type, which was sold to the military as the lwb RL and later became available for civilian users together with the swb RS. Production continued until 1969. In 1954, lorry and PSV production moved to a brand-new plant in nearby Dunstable, the largest of its type in Europe at the time. Production increased rapidly thereafter. In 1957, the TA Series was replaced by the improved TD Series and joined by the 4-ton/6-ton C Type, which used the revised S Type cab introduced simultaneously.

In 1959, the well-known bonneted J Type ('TJ') was launched, replacing the TD. Models were initially available rated from 30-cwt to 6 tons, and there was also an 8-ton tractor with Scammell coupling. These were joined by the 1960 replacement for the C and S Types, the equally well-known forward control TK, with its longitudinally-mounted engine below the rear of the driver's cab.

The KM range was added in 1966, using the TK-style cab – although otherwise it was a quite separate range – for vehicles up to 24 tons gvw. This introduced Bedford to the heavy end of the market for the first time. The 4x4 MK version replaced the RL/RS in 1969.

Although TKs had been available as tractors, in 1972 the KM 32-ton gcw tractor, with General Motors 'Detroit Diesel' two-stroke engine, more fully filled this niche. This was soon replaced by a model in the new TM range, which used a completely new high square cab, with narrow and wide versions, plus sleeper options, for use on six-wheeled rigids and tractor units from 24-32 tons gross, also using the Detroit Diesel engine. This range took Bedford into the maximum weight category for the first time, with some measure of success. Four and six-wheeled military derivatives of the TM were also introduced.

The bonneted TJ Series sold consistently well in overseas markets, for which it remained in production until 1986 as the JM range (although Dunstable ceased production in 1975 for the domestic market). In 1978, the TJ 4x2 and 6x2 range was extended from 5 tons to 16 tons gvw.

In March 1980, the tilt-cab TL range was offered at last as an intended successor to the TK, although this continued in production. The TL ranged from 5.69 tonnes gvw through to 16.3 tonnes, with two tractor units at 16.26 and 19.3 tonnes gcw, the model designation being derived from gross weight.

In 1983, the Bedford truck division was transferred to a new US company, General Motors Overseas Commercial Vehicle Corporation, a subsidiary of General Motors' Worldwide Truck & Bus Group in Pontiac, Michigan. However, the first stages of recession were beginning to hit the motor industry generally, and in 1985 there were voluntary redundancies. The company was making massive losses. Most Bedford models were slowly discontinued until, in 1986, a decision was made to pull out of the heavy-vehicle market apart from military vehicles, mainly of the TM 6x6 type.

In November 1987, Bedford was sold to a British concern. AWD (All Wheel Drive) Ltd acquired the Dunstable plant and the rights to the Bedford truck and bus range which had been discontinued in 1986. The intention was to market some of the Bedford TL, TK and TM range but to concentrate on military contracts and four and six-wheel drive vehicles. However, by June 1992 it was announced that AWD was in the hands of the receivers.

AWD had lost out to Leyland DAF in a competition to supply replacements for the Ministry of Defence

Above: This 8-ton OSS Bedford-Scammell tractor was registered in Newport, Monmouthshire, having been purchased new by well-known heavy haulier Wynn's of Newport in 1947/8. It was photographed in 1949, delivering a Terrapin mobile dwelling which, in combination with other units, took two hours in a demonstration to create a four-roomed house. *Ian Allan Library*

fleet of M Type Bedfords. Consequently the new manufacturer's dream of producing 8,000 trucks for the MoD was unrealised. Indeed, over the five years of its existence, AWD sold fewer trucks to British civilian operators than Bedford had done in its last year as a General Motors subsidiary.

Later in 1992, the Cambridge-based Marshall group purchased the production, tooling and design rights to the AWD range, resuming production the following February at much lower volumes. The commercial-vehicle business became part of Marshall SPV (Special Purpose Vehicles) – an assortment of commercial-vehicle chassis and body-building businesses gathered into aircraft hangars. The AWD operation was transferred to Cambridge ready for the resumption of production.

Initially lorries, particularly TLs, were sold with Marshall badging, although, as GM had rebadged all light commercials as Vauxhalls, Marshall was also able to acquire the rights to the Bedford name. However, there were only a few sales, and the marque was doomed.

In 1997, Marshall unveiled the prototype of its Utility Truck, offered with a choice of Cummins B or C Series engine and fitted with a brand new cab. However, in May 1999 the rights to the Utility Truck's cab, the

Bedford parts business and a bus design were all sold by Marshall Specialist Purpose Vehicles to ERF Ltd of Middlewich, Cheshire (see ERF, page 64). ERF then appointed Associated Vehicle Industries Ltd of Dunstable to operate as the Bedford Direct Export Sales Centre. By then, production of the Bedford truck range had already ground to a halt. The last TL to be sold in the UK was a 1996-built TL17-18, which had been retained as a display vehicle at the Marshall factory. It was sold in 2001 by Croft Bros, a dealership in Uxbridge, to Willies Wheels and fitted out as a mobile generating unit for use in the film industry.

After ERF was acquired by MAN Commercial Vehicles in 2000, the Amethyst Group Ltd of Staplehurst, Kent, purchased the Bedford Genuine Parts business in 2002. Amethyst continues to provide logistics support to ERF/MAN.

Above: The second prototype De Havilland Comet 1 G-ALZK was delivered on 2 April 1951 for 500 flying hours of crew training and route proving from Hatfield Aerodrome to the BOAC Comet Unit at Hurn (now Bournemouth) Airport, then in Hampshire, where this 17 May 1952 shot is believed to have been taken. De Havilland's 1951-registered Bedford 5-ton OSB was used by the Airspeed Division at Portsmouth Airport. *Vauxhall Motors*

Left: This 1952-registered 30mph-restricted Bedford-Scammell OSS had a ulw of 2 tons 1-cwt 2qrt 21lb. It was coupled in this August 1953 view to a 32ft articulated drop-frame van trailer, making several trips a day transporting materials and finished products between the Huddersfield and Barnsley factories of Brook Motors Ltd of Huddersfield. *Brook Motors Ltd*

Right: The 'Big Bedford' or S Type forward control was introduced in 1951, built initially in Luton and then, from 1954, at the new Dunstable truck plant. This 7-ton swb SS (the lwb model was the SL) from the Stanbridge (Luton) Ltd fleet was one of the first standard tippers delivered and had an all-steel 6 cu yd body. The ulw was less than three tons. *Ian Allan Library*

Below: The normal control TA Series appeared in early 1953, replacing the K and O Types. Capacities were 30-cwt, then 3, 4 and 5 tons with swb and lwb, plus an 8-ton Scammell coupling tractor unit. Seen here in Newport, Isle of Wight, is the early TA dropside of local fruit and potato merchant Reg Wells Ltd. *Ian Allan Library*

Right: In 1957, the revised TD Series replaced the TA with 30-cwt, 2, 3, 4, 5 and 6-ton swb and lwb versions, plus an 8-ton Scammell coupling tractor unit. This TD rigid box van, No 803 in the fleet of Unilever subsidiary SPD (Speedy Prompt Delivery), was photographed when new in February 1958. *Ian Allan Library*

Right: Lacre had produced vehicles under its own name in the early part of the 20th century, but latterly concentrated on roadsweepers. By the 1950s, its equipment was being mounted on other makers' chassis. This is a left-hand-drive late-'50s Bedford TD, most likely a D2S two-tonner, fitted with a Lacre roadsweeping body. *CHC abe202*

Right: The S Type was revised in 1957, and was joined by the lighter 4, 5 and 6-ton C Types that shared the S Type cab. This shot from December 1957 shows a petrol-engined Bedford-Scammell model SA with a refrigerated van trailer, in service with food wholesalers/importers John Connell (Bromley) Ltd. Diesel engines were an option by then, as with the other normal and forward control models. *Ian Allan Library*

Left: In 1951, Bedford started production of the 4x4 R Type, derivative of the S Type, initially intended for military applications. Production continued to 1969, when it was replaced by the MK version of the TK; in due course, diesel engines also became an option. Both the swb RS and lwb RL chassis were offered as commercial models, as shown by this March 1958 shot of a Southern Electricity Service RSH with auxiliary engine-powered equipment in the back. Note the revised cab used from 1957, shared with the C and S types. Chassis-cowl 'Z'-suffixed versions were also offered. *Ian Allan Library*

Left: This RL with RLH standard single rear wheels – duals and heavy-duty suspension being optional – has earth-boring equipment for the erection of wooden poles by Cheshire Highway Utilities Ltd of Camberley, Surrey. It was in the fleet of Colets Earth Boring & Plant Hire Ltd of Bookham, Surrey. *Vauxhall Motors*

Left: The well-known normal control TJ or J Series appeared in 1959, as represented by this April 1959 shot of a swb 6-ton J6S (a J6L lwb was also available). The diesel badge confirms it has the 300 cu in Bedford diesel option. It also has a 6 cu yd tipper body and a heavy-duty two-speed axle. It was in the fleet of George C. Cross & Co Ltd of Southall, Middlesex. *Vauxhall Motors*

Right: The forward control TK Series was launched in September 1960, with 3 to 7-ton rigids and 8, 10 and 12-ton tractor units. This 17 December 1960 shot shows the 100,000th Bedford built that year (a record), which was a lwb TJ chassis-cab. The year's end total was 106,284 with a £136 million turnover. Note the two J4A 8-ton Bedford-Scammell tractors behind it, plus several TKs (including tractors) and an SB PSV chassis (also used for fire engines and pantechnicons).
Vauxhall Motors

Left: The TK range became available in due course with 6x2 and 6x4 conversions including the Bedford-Boughton conversion from Reynolds-Boughton, as shown here on a 1967-registered tipper. As No 178 in service with Manchester brick manufacturer J. & A. Jackson Ltd, it had a ulw of 6 tons 16-cwt 2qrt.
Ian Allan Library

Left: The Bedford KM was introduced in 1966. It was a similar vehicle to the TK, using the same cab (or with an optional deluxe cab) but with a slightly restyled front end with twin bumpers and headlights, marketed for heavier-duty applications than the TK at 16 tons gross and over. Believed to be the first light-alloy refrigerated body on the longest wheelbase KM (224 in, model KMH), it was part of the fleet of Bonallack Refrigerated Vehicles Ltd, designed to carry a 9½-ton palletised load and containing a Thermo King refrigerator unit. *Vauxhall Motors*

Left: The MK 4x4, based on the TK, replaced the RS/RL, to suit the Ministry of Defence's requirement for an RL replacement. The 4-ton MK went into service with the British Army in 1969 and a commercial version followed. This shot, taken in the late 1970s, shows a Tico K1000 Hydraulic Lorry Loader. The military MJ with diesel engine replaced the multi-fuel MK in April 1981, later being produced by AWD. *Ian Allan Library*

Left: The Bedford TM was manufactured between 1974 and 1986, designed as a competitor to the European vehicles then becoming popular. It was offered as either an articulated tractor unit or as a rigid, with either wide or narrow day and sleeper cabs. This October 1977 view is of a TM 3800 tractor, one of five with Scottish & Newcastle Breweries Ltd. Although designed to haul 38 tonnes, it was rated at the time at 32 tons. A sleeper-cab 3800 was exhibited at the 1977 Scottish Motor Show. The heaviest model, the TM 4400, was rated at 44 tonnes gtw for the export market, fitted with a 380bhp GM Detroit-Diesel 8V-92TT engine. *Vauxhall Motors*

Right: This shot, taken in May 1978, shows a TM tractor converted to an lwb six-wheeled rigid for Northampton printer Clarke & Sherwell Ltd by York Trailer Co Ltd. *York Trailer Co*

Right: By 1981, the TK was joined (and eventually largely replaced) by the TL, though the new tilt-cab model did not prove as popular as the non-tilt TK Series had been. This February 1982 shot shows three of 35 TLs ordered by BRS Truck Rental. That on the left is a 16-ton TL1630 chassis, while the other two are non-HGV TL860 chassis. *Vauxhall Motors*

Right: The Bedford stand for the 1982 Commercial Motor Show at the NEC, Birmingham, had several models on display, including various TLs (four in view here) plus one TK – as well as TJ, KM 4x4 and TM chassis-cabs. There was also a TM 4x4 on a separate stand. *CHC abg406*

Above: The 1983 model year saw the introduction of lorries with new turbocharged engines as standard, plus revised cabs with new trim and seating. This 16-tonne TL 1630 with a tipper body also has improved axles and more efficient direct-drive gearbox. *Vauxhall Motors*

Left: A number of Bedford operators were able to continue buying vehicles badged 'AWD' when this company took over production after General Motors closed its European lorry-building operations. The vehicles produced included these TL10-14 chassis fitted with scissor-lift bodywork for an airport catering company. *Tony Croft/AWD*

BMC

The British Motor Corporation, usually known as BMC, was formed by the 1952 merger of the Austin Motor Company and the Nuffield Organisation, parent company of Morris Motors Ltd – which included Morris cars and light commercials, as well as Morris Commercial Cars Ltd of Adderley Park, Birmingham, MG, Riley, Wolseley and numerous other companies.

The Austin and Morris light commercials were rationalised over the next few years. 'Morris-Commercial' badging was dropped in favour of 'Morris' by 1957, and until 1968 identical commercials were offered as either Austin or Morris-badged versions through their respective independent dealerships. By 1956, heavy commercials were being built at Austin Motors, Longbridge, once again badged as 'Austin' or 'Morris' although some bore 'BMC' – including the 7-ton forward control lorries sold by either Austin or Morris commercial dealerships.

The FG/FM Series was built at Alderley Park from 1960-62. The new Bathgate, West Lothian plant opened in 1960, with production of the heavier lorries, including the BMC-badged seven-tonners, moving there from Longbridge and Alderley Park (FG/FM) for the 1963 model year.

The lorry models in the 1960s included the FF, a forward control design introduced in 1958, along with the normal control WF (1955-64) with Loadstar-derived cab – a basically similar vehicle, although the driver was positioned behind the engine

rather than on top of it. The 1964-68 updated version of the FF, the FJ, appeared in 1964, featuring one of the first tilt-cabs in the UK plus split-circuit braking system, a novelty in this class of vehicle. The FF still remained in production for a time and the two vehicles were offered side by side. However, in this class the BMC trucks could not compete in terms of the domestic market sales of Bedford and Ford.

After the British Motor Corporation merged with Leyland Motors Ltd in 1968, the BMC name was used for two years on lorries such as the WF, FG, Laird and the VA 'Noddy Van' for BRS Parcels, but was replaced by Leyland badging from 1970 onwards. The larger vehicles were rebadged as 'Leyland', joining its existing range, while the light commercials became 'Austin Morris'

In 1964, the British Motor Corporation went into partnership with Ergün Özakatin Izmir, Turkey, which produced BMC vehicles under licence during its early years. In 1966, BMC begn to add truck, light truck, tractor and engine production to its Turkish product range. In 1989, the company was fully acquired by Cukurova Holding of Turkey. In recent years some BMC-badged school buses have been imported, thus perpetuating the name in the UK.

Right: From 1955, the Longbridge-built Austin and Morris FE (Series III) acquired a corporate front-end design, and the new seven-tonner was badged as 'BMC' only, though it was sold by either Austin or Morris commercial-vehicle dealers. This shot dates from June 1956 and shows a BMC diesel-engined tipper, No 22 in the fleet of Samuel Wilkinson & Sons Ltd of Blackely Fireclay Works at Elland, Yorkshire. *Ian Allan Library*

Left: This diesel-engined FE platform-bodied rigid four-wheeler was photographed in May 1958. It was in the fleet of Dunford & Elliott (Sheffield) Ltd, maker of Dunelt Sheffield steels. *Ian Allan Library*

Above: After the 1968 BMC and Leyland Motors merger, the FJ cab was given a mild makeover. Now known as the Pilot cab, it formed the basis of the BMC Laird and Terrier light trucks, with the twin headlamps replaced by singles in pods. The new series was available in three rigid chassis versions, with five wheelbase lengths, and as a Prime Mover or tractor unit. The engines were either 5.1 or 5.7-litre units. The Pilot cab vehicles were rebadged as 'Leyland' in 1970, and replaced in 1975 by the Leyland G Series. *BMC Commercials*

Above: From 1964-68, the Bathgate-built Austin/Morris FJ could be bought as either an Austin or a Morris, with non-HGV ratings of 5 or 7 tons and BMC-badged heavier versions, including the 8-ton K160 and the 10-ton K360 Prime Mover. This view of a six-wheeled tipper dates to March 1966 and shows Tarmac Roadstone Ltd's No 32/167. Note the lack of a BMC badge. *Ian Allan Library*

BRISTOL

The Bristol Tramways & Carriage Co, founded in 1887, started running motor buses in 1906 in the Bristol area and then built its own chassis in Brislington from 1908, including a few lorries. From the early 1930s it became part of the Tilling Group of operators, and, as a result, other operators in the group started to standardise on Bristol chassis, usually bodied by another Tilling company, Eastern Counties (later Eastern Coach Works). In 1947, the Tilling Group, including Bristol and ECW, was nationalised. Restrictions were soon imposed, so that Bristol and ECW could only supply to other subsidiaries of the British Transport Commission (BTC).

Following nationalisation of a large number of road transport companies from 1948, the goods haulage arm of the BTC, the Road Haulage Executive (which included BRS) needed to re-equip with new lorries. In 1952, Bristol introduced a 22-ton gross (the heaviest permitted at the time) eight-wheeled heavy goods chassis, fitted with the 125bhp 9.8-litre Leyland O.600 diesel engine. The HG6L model used Bristol's own gearbox, transmission and other components. A total of 517 was built in the end, some differing in appearance, as cabs from several different body-builders were used.

As the demands from BRS changed, in 1955 an articulated tractor-unit model, the HA6L (also fitted with with the O.600 engine) was introduced. This later became the HA6G, when Gardner engines were used, and the HA6GX, when the more-powerful 6LX engine was introduced. Bristol also built a matching 24ft semi-trailer, designated as the ST.

The manufacturing arm of the Bristol Tramways & Carriage Co became Bristol Commercial Vehicles Ltd in 1955. However, the company would stop building commercial vehicles in 1964, although bus chassis continued.

Bristol was released from its restriction of sales to state-owned operators in 1965. This came about via the Government's swapping some shares with Leyland and the company being denationalised. Later, Bristol became part of Bus Manufacturers (Holdings) Ltd, which was a joint undertaking between the state-owned British Leyland Motor Corporation and the National Bus Company. After only a thousand Leyland-badged Olympian chassis had been built, Leyland – by now in sole charge of Bristol – closed the Brislington factory in October 1983.

Right: The Bristol HG6L was the first commercial chassis built by Bristol Tramways & Carriage Co since the 1920s. Introduced in 1952, the eight-wheel rigid chassis was built exclusively for the Road Haulage Executive of the British Road Services (BRS) fleet. Total production was 517 units, using different styles of cabs built by several subcontractors. In 1955, Bristol chassis production was separated from the bus operating activities and renamed Bristol Commercial Vehicles. Initially, the lorries ran at 22 tons, the legal maximum, and then later 24 tons. This 1955-registered Bristol-cabbed example was BRS No 43A610. It appears to be in Central London, with a typical tarpaulin-covered load on the platform body.
Ian Allan Library

Above: The 24-ton HA6L Leyland-engined articulated tractor unit was available from 1955, together with the 24ft ST semi-trailer. This is an early example, with the revolutionary Bristol all glass-fibre cab, manufactured from 1960 by Longwell Green Coachworks. *Bristol Commercial Vehicles*

Below: This is a later HA6G tractor unit with a Gardner 6LX engine. BRS No 1A980 was new in late 1963 and had the later Longwell Green cab design. Total tractor unit production was 653. Note the load of boxes of Heinz canned products ready to be sheeted up. *CHC aab260*

COMMER

Commercial Cars Ltd was founded in 1905 and moved to Biscot Road, Luton, Bedfordshire, in 1907, whereupon the name was abbreviated to Commer. The company had a chequered career. After going into receivership it was taken over by Humber Cars, which itself became part of the Rootes Group in November 1928. In the autumn of 1934, Commer acquired Karrier Motors (Successors) Ltd of Huddersfield through Humber Ltd and moved production to Biscot Road, alongside Commer in a modernised plant.

During World War 2, Commer built over 20,000 vehicles for the armed forces. When peace resumed, the pre-war normal control Superpoise restarted production, supplemented by a Commer-Hands 6 to 8-ton tractor and semitrailer outfit, with a new style of cab also introduced. In 1948, a redesigned range with full forward control and underfloor engines called the QX was put on the market for 5-ton and 7-ton payloads. From 1951, the 3-ton Q4 4x4 military lorry was a derivative of the Superpoise. This range was further extended in 1955 by 2 to 5-ton vehicles with a six-cylinder diesel engine, while a new normal control cab was manufactured by Airflow Streamlines which was also used by Dodge and others.

Production facilities were outdated at Biscot Road, so a new assembly plant was opened in Dunstable, Bedfordshire in 1955, coinciding with Commer's 50th anniversary. All Commer and Karrier production

moved there, including the 7-ton lwb QX previously assembled at Rootes' Stoke Aldermoor, Coventry plant. Biscot Road continued to build gearboxes and back axles as well as continuing with model development. A new two-stroke diesel engine called the TS3 (originally designed by Tilling-Stevens, now also part of the Rootes Group) was marketed in 1953, with two horizontally-opposed pistons in each of the three cylinders. This engine was fitted to certain vehicles of the range, but alternative Perkins diesel engines of conventional design were also offered.

The 30-cwt to 3-ton Walk-Thru delivery van with semi-forward control was introduced in 1961, its style clearly carrying a lot of US influence. The Maxiload 12-ton tractor unit joined the range in 1962 and, in 1966, Commer entered the heavier market with a 16-ton gcw chassis and cab. The same style of cab also appeared on the C Series range of forward control mediumweight

Below: This shot is dated November 1945 and shows a Commer-Hands articulated tractor-trailer for 8-ton loads. Note how the cab carries the legend 'K. Harlow – East Peckham, Kent' and the trailer 'C. Harlow – London Spitalfields Market', suggesting it was used between Kent and the City market. The pre-war Commando formed the basis of the post-war (Mk I) Superpoise Q Series ranging from 2/3-6½ tons. The pre-war N and LN Series also carried over. *Commer Cars*

vehicles in 1963, which were later superseded by the outwardly similar V Series.

In 1964, the US Chrysler Corporation acquired a financial interest in the cash-strapped Rootes Group. In 1965, all commercial vehicle production moved from Luton to Dunstable, bringing together Commer, Karrier and Dodge (already part of Chrysler and previously based at Kew, Surrey). In January 1967, the Chrysler Corporation expanded its shareholding in the Rootes Group to 77.3%; by 1968 it had total ownership. Vehicles were now being marketed under the name Rootes Motors Limited (Commer/Karrier Division), but by 1970 this changed to Chrysler United Kingdom Ltd (Commer/Karrier Division).

The Commer Commando range was launched in February 1974. It appears that the Commer name was dropped from August 1976 in favour of Dodge, although badging of the PB light vans does not seem to have changed until January 1977.

In 1978, the French company PSA (Peugeot-Citroën) reached agreement with Chrysler Corporation for the purchase and takeover of Chrysler's principal European operations. The Karrier name resurfaced occasionally on certain municipal market vehicles, as seen in the section on Dodge (see page 55).

Below: A new cab was introduced for the Mk II Superpoise in 1948. This dropside lorry was in use by the Zoological Society of London's Whipsnade Zoo near Dunstable. *Commer Cars*

Left: The new 5 to 7-ton forward control QX range was introduced in 1948. Photographed in Central London's Long Acre in September 1950 – just around the corner from Covent Garden fruit, vegetable and flower markets – is Continental Fruits' late 1949-registered QX with unusual Oaklands Motor Bodies Ltd of Bristol bodywork. Seen in the background, National Provincial Bank would merge with the Westminster Bank to form the National Westminster Bank (now NatWest) in 1970. *Ian Allan Library*

44

Right: In 1955 the Superpoise range received a facelift with a new front design, introducing the Mk IV (the Mk III debuted in 1951 and Mk IIIA in 1954) which lasted until 1962. These 1957 Mk IV 3-4-ton vans supplied to matchmaker S. J. Moreland & Sons Ltd of Gloucester had 600 cu ft-capacity aluminium-alloy bodies with wooden floors, manufactured by Longwell Green Coachworks. The ulw was just under 3 tons. *Commer Cars*

Below: The QX was updated in 1956, with chrome flashes and enlarged Commer badge on the (Rootes Group) British Light Steel Pressings Ltd cab. This late 1957-registered TS3 diesel-engined tractor was in service with the Kent-based Hercules Powder Co Ltd, its fleet based in Park Lane, London W1. *Ian Allan Library*

Left: The QX received its final update in 1958 and continued until 1963. The revised front end and single-piece windscreen are clearly visible. This TS3-engined seven-tonner was loaded to a gvw of 10 tons 16-cwt and is seen splashing through the mud at the Motor Industry Research Association (MIRA), near Nuneaton. *Rootes Motors*

Right: The CA was launched for 1962 as an eight-tonner and used a Sankey of Birmingham cab, as did the new VA four, five, six and seven-tonners and the Karrier Gamecock four, five and six-tonners (albeit with single headlamps). The CB/VB replaced the CA/VA in 1964 and the CC/VC in 1965, lasting until 1973. This CA8 was photographed in July 1962 en route from Smithfield Meat Market in the City of London, in the fleet of Lea & Baxter Ltd of Northampton. It had an insulated Litex body built by Smiths Delivery Vehicles Ltd of Gateshead-on-Tyne. *Ian Allan Library*

Left: In 1959 Commer Cars produced some multi-fuel QX seven-tonners for a UK military contract (won by the Bedford TK) and for overseas customers. This shot was taken in November 1959, when the vehicle was possibly destined for France. Commer went on to produce multi-fuel military vehicles based on the CA Series. *Rootes Motors*

Right: The Commer (or Karrier, for municipal markets) Walk-Thru was introduced in 1961 and was also produced as a Dodge until 1977. This 1962-registered van was used by Hoveringham as a service van for its tipper fleet.
Rootes Motors

Right: By spring 1965, Dodges were being sold as Commers and Commers as Dodges. This October 1966 shot is of a 6-ton LA.6 low-loader with the Dodge K Series tilt-cab. Engines were either 130bhp V6 or 120bhp in-line diesel.
Rootes Motors

Right: This VC was new in summer 1970, seen here at a SBAC Farnborough Air Show in the early 1970s. It had a Houchin 'Super Power' ground power unit for starting aircraft.
CHC aai956

DENNIS

1904-present

John Dennis began by building cycles in 1885, and later brought his younger brother Raymond into the rapidly expanding business. It was a logical step from cycles to the early motorcycles – called Speed Kings – and then on to motorcars. Dennis Bros of Guildford produced its first commercial vehicle in 1904 and had two 14hp two-cylinder models plus 20, 24 and 28hp four-cylinder vehicles available two years later. Fire engine production started as early as 1908, while one year earlier the company had produced its first worm-drive 5-ton lorry.

The War Department's 3-ton subsidy lorry of 1913 was produced in large numbers and, afterward, the similar 2-ton chassis proved popular for municipal vehicles such as refuse collectors, gully emptiers, cesspool emptiers and so on.

By 1918, Dennis had acquired the well-known Coventry engine manufacturer White and Poppe, but did not enter the heavy commercial market until the 1920s. Even in the 1930s, Dennis was concentrating on the 2 to 6-ton range, with the exception of a six-wheeled 12-tonner introduced in 1931. In 1933, Dennis produced its popular Ace models, which became known as 'Flying Pigs' because of the protruding snout-like bonnet ahead of the front axle. A heavier vehicle, called the Max, appeared in 1937 with a payload of 6-7 tons and full-forward control. Wartime production included large numbers of trailer fire pumps and various vehicles for the services.

Production resumed in 1946 with the Max, plus the Pax five-tonner. A new 12-ton six-wheeled chassis was added called the Jubilant, which had a five-speed gearbox and a 7.6-litre engine, later enlarged to eight litres. The latter engine also powered the Centaur forward control 6 to 7-ton rigid lorry, introduced in 1948, and the 12-ton Horla tractor unit.

In 1954, Dennis introduced a newly designed 3-ton payload van with an underfloor engine called the Stork; this was later joined by the Paravan, but neither appears to have been as popular as it deserved to be. The Max was replaced by the Hefty in 1957, while the Centaur gave way to the Condor for the hauling of 7-ton payloads. The heavy market from 1964 onward was supplied with the Maxim, available as a four-wheeled rigid 16-tonner, a similar six-wheeled 22-ton gvw vehicle and a tractor unit for up to 30 tons gcw; again, none of these models appear to have been very successful. Throughout this period, however, the production rate of fire appliances and municipal refuse collectors, many of them using the company's Paxit compression system, was considerable.

At a time when Dennis was experiencing a downturn in the bus-building side of its business and fewer sales of commercial vehicles, it was acquired in 1972 by the Hestair Group. The company injected capital into the organisation, which subsequently became Hestair Dennis. Under Hestair ownership,

Left: The Friary Brewery in Guildford, Surrey was founded in 1868. After mergers, Friary, Holroyd and Healy's Breweries Ltd was incorporated in 1895. In 1956, it merged with the Meux Brewery to form Friary Meux Ltd. Friary also acquired Guildford-built Dennis brewery drays, and this new four-wheeled Max was photographed in September 1946. *Ian Allan Library*

Dennis began to re-establish itself as a leading bus and coach chassis manufacturer while continuing to supply fire appliances and municipal vehicles.

During the mid-to-late 1970s, the company's focus was on establishing a completely new passenger range. However, in 1979, the Delta 16-ton freight chassis for tipper and general haulage applications was revitalised, going into fullscale production with a new metal cab – albeit in smaller quantities than those of most other manufacturers. Like other contemporary models in the Dennis range, it was available with a wide range of engine/gearbox options.

The old plant at Guildford was first slimmed down and then replaced, during the 1980s, by a brand-new factory a couple of miles away. However, Hestair sold its commercial vehicle business to a management team called Trinity Holdings in 1989, who later renamed the business the Dennis Group. When it had acquired Dennis, Hestair also owned Eagle Engineering, a refuse-body and tanker manufacturer, and so the two businesses were renamed Hestair Dennis and Hestair Eagle respectively; after the management buy-out, they would become Dennis Specialist Vehicles and Dennis Eagle.

Production of complete refuse vehicles, chassis, cabs and bodies, was moved to a new Eagle factory in Warwick in 1985. Fire appliance bodywork was sub-contracted.

Production of the Delta truck came to an end in 1983, when Dennis concluded that its future lay in the more promising municipal vehicle, fire appliance and bus markets; its small production runs of haulage trucks, although Calor Gas was a high-profile customer, was too low to be economically justifiable.

Fire-appliance development took a step forward, in 1991, with the launch of the new Rapier, an integral construction vehicle with coil-spring rear suspension and a low centre of gravity. This was followed by the less sophisticated Sabre, with separate chassis but similar cab styling; the same cab styling was also used for the Dennis Eagle Elite refuse truck, launched in 1992.

Towards the end of 1998, Dennis changed hands again when it was acquired by the Mayflower Corporation, a British engineering group with growing automotive interests. The main attraction for Mayflower was Dennis's bus and coach business, which fitted with its existing bus-body building activities, but it also retained the fire appliance business. Dennis became part of Mayflower Bus & Coach, and then later TransBus International. When the Mayflower Group went into administration in 2004, Transbus was bought out and became Alexander Dennis.

Prior to this, in July 1999, Mayflower had sold Dennis Eagle along with two other specialist vehicle subsidiaries: Douglas Equipment and Schopf Maschinhenbau. Dennis Eagle is still based in Warwick, where it produces refuse-collection vehicles and chassis for specialist units, such as airport refuellers and motorway-service vehicles. Dennis Specialist Vehicles is still in Guildford and still manufacturing fire engines, as well as bus chassis.

Today, Dennis Eagle Ltd is at the Heathcote Industrial Estate in Warwick. Its 2012 models include the Olympus, Beta 2, Twin Pack, Duo, One Pass RCVs (refuse collection vehicles) and the Elite 2 chassis-cab range.

Above: This view, taken in September 1950, is of a BRS furniture van with an Arlington light-alloy pantechnicon body on a 5-ton Pax chassis. *Ian Allan Library*

Left: Coming off the line on 17 December 1955 is a modern-style Heron tractor unit, followed by a more traditional fire engine. The Perkins-engined Heron debuted at the November 1955 Scottish Motor Show and was available as a four-wheeled rigid, among other models. *Ian Allan Library*

Right: No review of Dennis vehicles would be complete without the Paravan parcels van, introduced in 1958. This is an early example in the well-known fleet of Essex Carriers Ltd of South Benfleet, which had a hand in its design. *Ian Allan Library*

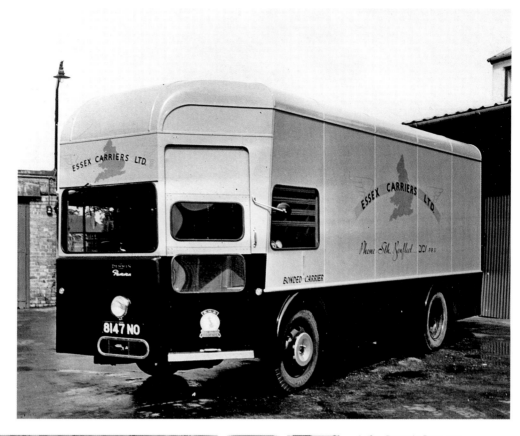

Left: Dennis Bros are synonymous with refuse-collecting vehicles. This 1963 model Paxit IIIa was on the Dennis stand at the 1962 Commercial Show, with an automatic, continuous-loading, refuse collection body. *CHC aao089*

Left: The Dennis Maxim was launched in 1964. It was powered by a Cummins V8 of 185hp, and intended for the then new 32-ton gross weight limit. However, the Cummins V8 was apparently unsatisfactory in this application and, from 1966, the Maxim was re-engineered with a 170bp Perkins V8 510 engine as a 30-tonner with an acclaimed payload of 21 tons, rivalling that of a five-axle 32-tonner. The Maxim was advertised as a two or three-seat GRP-cabbed 20 to 32-ton tractor and also as a three-axle rigid. This shot dates from June 1967. *Dennis Bros Ltd*

Right: The Pax V was the 1960s replacement for the Pax IV; it was available as shown here (in September 1968) as a tractor, or as a four-wheeled rigid, tipper and van. *Ian Allan Library*

Right: This 1982/3 four-wheeler had a refrigerated insulated body and was on the fleet of Leicester Market-based meat specialist W. & J. Parker (Wholesale) Ltd. *PM Photography*

Left: Typical of the higher-capacity refuse-collection vehicles used by local authority contractors in recent years, this mid-1990s six-wheeled Dennis on the Direct Services fleet is seen working for North Wiltshire District Council. *Michelin*

Below: One of the latest traffic management vehicles delivered to VOSA in 2010, this Dennis six-wheeler uses the same cab as the latest refuse collection vehicles from the same company. *Dennis Specialist Vehicles*

DENNISON

1964-present

Dennison Trailers, which is still a family-owned and run business, began in Northern Ireland in 1964 by making flatbed trailers. The company then moved to a site just outside Dublin in 1970. In 1983, the current manufacturing plant was opened in Naas, County Kildare; six years later, to serve the UK market, Dennison opened a further plant in Caton Road, Lancaster.

Dennison Ltd's lorry-making business was founded in Rathcoole, Dublin, in 1977, after Dennison Trailers was sold to Crane Fruefauf. The lorries were built from parts supplied by several OEM suppliers, initially with cabs from Motor Panels, engines from Rolls-Royce Eagle (265bhp) or Gardner (240bhp) and Fuller gearboxes with Eaton axles. From 1979, Sisu cabs from Finland were used in the Mk2 models, which also had the 290 Rolls-Royce option.

Most were sold into the Irish market, but a few were exported to the UK. Dennison's London dealer was AM Western Ltd, which ran at least one demonstrator. By 1981, after building nearly 250 trucks, the company ceased their manufacture and went back to building trailers at a new factory near Dublin (as Dennison Trailers Ltd). Dennison built 4x2 and 6x2 tractors and 8x4 rigids, mainly for tipper use. The company has several examples of trucks and trailers in its museum at the Naas production site in Ireland.

Left: This Dennison tractor unit was tested by *Commercial Motor* on the road and at MIRA, near Nuneaton. It had the 265bhp Rolls-Royce Eagle engine. Note the Crane Fruehauf trailer and test load. *CHC aac471*

Left: This 1981 eight-wheeler tipper has clearly seen some service! It was owned by P. & R. Bushell Ltd of Heather Mount, Halkyn, Flintshire. *PM Photography*

DODGE

1922-93

The US company Dodge Bros first began assembling imported parts in the UK in 1922, through its subsidiary Dodge Bros (Britain) Ltd, at Fulham, South-West London, then at Park Royal in North-West London in 1925. After the Chrysler Corporation acquired Dodge Bros in 1928, the company's second subsidiary was the successor to Maxwell Motors Ltd, becoming Maxwell-Chrysler Ltd and then Chrysler Motors Ltd in 1925, with an assembly plant in Kew, Surrey.

Dodge was then moved to the Kew plant and started manufacturing British chassis in 1933. The company used US or Canadian side-valve six-cylinder engines and gearboxes, as well as Perkins oil engines. During World War 2, the plant assembled two models and also handled imported US/Canadian Dodges and Fargos for the military and essential civilian uses.

After the war, Kew recommenced production of its pre-war models. In 1949, Dodge introduced the 100 Series, which included the 103, 105 and 106 models, plus an articulated tractor unit and the 123, once again using either US/Canadian six-cylinder petrol or Perkins diesel engines. A seven-tonner was added in 1953. The chassis were fitted with a Briggs Motors Bodies Ltd cab similar to that used on the Leyland Comet and Fordson

Thames, with a ridged bonnet which led to the popular name 'Parrot-nose'.

In 1957, the 200 Series was introduced, with models in the 5, 7, 8 and 9-ton payload categories, plus 10 and 12-ton tractor unit models. There was also a four-wheel-drive five-tonner for off-highway or military applications. The normal control vehicles had cabs like the later Commer Superpoise, built by Airflow Streamlines.

In 1963, the 200 Series was replaced by the 400 with an American-style cab and Perkins engines. Most of the production was sent abroad before this model was discontinued, two years after its launch.

More popular from 1958 onwards, the Dodge 300 Series was a new range of forward control lorries ranging up to 20-ton gcw artics. These used the Motor Panels LAD cab shared with Albion and Leyland, with proprietary diesel engines from Perkins and others.

By the mid-1960s, Dodge Brothers had developed the Dodge 500 Series with a Ghia-designed tilt-cab to replace the 300. The Dodge 500 was designed for both UK and export markets. Like its predecessors, it was sold overseas as a Dodge, Fargo, De Soto or, from 1965, as a Commer after the Chrysler Corporation acquired a stake in Rootes Group. The Construction and Use

Right: The Kew Dodge Bros plant started commercial vehicle assembly immediately after World War 2, having previously handled imported North American lorries for governmental and municipal use. This semi-forward control with dropside body was registered in early 1946 and photographed in December that year, on the fleet of the British Oxygen Co Ltd (now BOC). It was used to transport bottled gases. *BOC*

Left: This Luton-style van used by racing driver F. R. Gerard was presumably supplied by the family business Parrs Ltd of Leicester (also ERF Distributors, which is now Bob Gerard Ltd). Contemporaries of Frederick Roberts Gerard called him the 'Gentleman of Motor Racing'. He competed in and won numerous trials, including the Ulster Trophy in 1947 and the British Empire Trophy on the Isle of Man on three separate occasions, going on to finish in second place at Silverstone in the 1949 British Grand Prix. *Ian Allan Library*

Regulations were significantly changed in 1964, with gross vehicle and gross combination weights increased to 16-28 tons or 22-32 tons respectively, depending on the chassis configuration. Axle loading was also increased in most applications and overall vehicle lengths were increased by 6-7ft. The styling of the new tilt cab was by Ghia of Turin, while the trucks were engineered at Kew with the help of many suppliers. The suspension used leaf springs in the front and rear, plus rear auxiliary springs as required. Their engines were the newly designed Chrysler-Cummins developed by Cummins for Europe – known as the VAL (V6) and VALE (V8), or Perkins 6.354 on lighter versions.

In 1967, the Kew plant closed and all production was moved to Commer/Karrier in Dunstable. By the end of the year, the site had been sold-off for development. The last lorries built at Kew were some 500-K100 tankers for Esso with Cummins V8 engines. Although Dodge Bros and Cummins had started their association in 1963, the Cummins engine was replaced in the 500 Series from January 1969 by the Perkins 510 V8.

In 1970, Rootes Motors Ltd changed its name to Chrysler UK Ltd; in July 1973, the Chrylser Corporation

Right: From 1949, for its new 100 Series, Dodge adopted the 'Parrot-nose' version of the cab built by Briggs Motor Bodies Ltd. Similar designs were used on the Leyland Comet and Fordson Thames, as well as by Guy Motors. The Briggs company was acquired by Ford in 1953. This 6-ton dropside was new in 1950 to Smedley's Ltd, which had a canned fruits factory in Wisbech, Cambridgeshire. *Ian Allan Library*

Right: The 100 Series included 2 to 3- and 5-ton petrol or diesel models, and 6-ton diesel 103, 105, and 106 models, plus an 8-ton articulated tractor unit (124A and 124A/P6 diesel). Later, a diesel seven-tonner was added in 1953 and various wheelbases were offered. The famous 1957 film *Hell Drivers* used Perkins-powered Dodge 123 dump trucks, similar to this 1955 tipper with side-valve six-cylinder petrol engine in the fleet of regular Dodge user W. W. Drinkwater Ltd, based in Taylors Lane, Willesden, North-West London, and with aggregates depots in Denham, Buckinghamshire (as featured here in June 1957), and Bushey Heath, Hertfordshire.
Ian Allan Library

acquired a 100% stake in the British company. The 1974-registered Commando was launched to replace existing Commer and Dodge models. From 1976 onwards, all Commer 7 to 12-ton Commandos were rebadged as 'Dodge', followed a few months later by the PB light vans and the Karrier Walk-Thru range. The Hi-line cab for the Commando re-introduced a tilt-cab. In September 1977, a 20-ton version of the G18 tractor was introduced, the 100 Series Commando G.2011P, which replaced the K500 Series 20 and 22-ton tractors. The K Series was eventually withdrawn in 1980.

In 1978, at the lighter end, the Walk-Thru was replaced by the American-styled 50 Series, covering the 3.5-7.5-tonne sector; the maximum-weight sector was covered by the 300 Series, imported from Chrysler's Spanish subsidiary Barreiros.

The Chrysler Corporation sold its European interests to PSA (Peugeot-Citroën) in 1978. The new French owner then sold the Dodge operations in England and Spain to Renault Vehicles Industriels in 1981. Renault Trucks Industries Ltd and PSA (Peugeot-Citroën) combined to form Karrier Motors Ltd, after which all Dodges then carried the Renault badge. In 1982, the Dodge range consisted of the 50 Series, the Spanish-built 300 Series and the 100 Series Commando,

revamped in 1981. Imports of the Barreiros 300 Series six and eight-wheeled rigids and maximum weight artic units stopped soon after the Renault takeover.

The sale of the business gave Renault limited rights to continue selling the trucks with Dodge badges, but Chrysler retained the trademark for use on cars, light commercials sold in the USA and in other markets. Renault began phasing out the Dodge name in the mid-1980s. Karrier Motors became Renault Truck Industries Ltd in 1983. In 1984, the first Dunstable-built Renault, the G260, was introduced. The new Commando 2 with restyled cab was sold alongside the Renault G170, R310, R310 Turboliner and the 50 Series.

Production of the Commando continued at Dunstable. It was given a final facelift in 1987, by which time all vehicles were badged as Renaults. In 1989, Renault started assembling French-designed Midliner lorries as the last Renault Commando rolled off the line in October that year. After Renault acquired Mack Trucks in 1991, it was decided to close down Dunstable. The company changed its name in December that year to Renault VI United Kingdom Ltd. The last Renault 50 and Midliner were completed in March 1993, ending assembly of British-built Renaults. However, the Vehicle Engineering Centre at Boscombe Road continued to adapt and modify Renault lorries for some time.

Above: The normal control Kew Dodge 200 Series used a cab very similar to the 1955-registered Commer Mk IV Superpoise. By 1957, these were being assembled at Kew alongside the forward control 300 Series. Latham's new 7-ton Dodge-Scammell tractor is captioned as a model 243 AY and photographed in November 1957 outside the Two Gates Garage, a Coventry car and commercials (including Perkins diesels) dealership and Mobil franchise. In 1963, the 200 Series was replaced by the 400 with an American-style cab. Most of the production was sent abroad before it was discontinued, two years after its launch. *Ian Allan Library*

Left: The forward control LAD cab was shared between Leyland, Albion and Dodge for its 300 Series. This 7-ton tractor with Perkins R6(V) Mk II engine was new to the fleet of G. A. Slater Ltd of Crowland, Lincolnshire, in 1958. Note the York dropside two-axle trailer. *Ian Allan Library*

Right: This 1962-registered 8-ton Dodge 300 Series fitted with a Perkins 6.354 engine was operated by W. Freeman & Sons, a Birmingham dairy. The 300 Series was available in 5, 7, 8 and 9-ton payload categories, plus 10 and 12-ton tractor models. There was also a four-wheel drive five-tonner for off-highway or military applications. *F. Perkins Ltd*

Left: The Dodge (and De Soto/Fargo, for export) 500 Series went into production in December 1964, having been developed in the early 1960s as a heavy-duty lorry intended for moving payloads in the UK and its export markets. This model KL600 10 to 12-ton gvw low-loader dates from September 1965. *Rootes Motors*

Left: From 1965, Commmer/Karrier started building Dodges in Dunstable. This 500-K1100 2,800-gallon Esso tanker was one of 44, among the last built at Kew before it closed in 1967, with a Cummins V8 engine and Allison automatic transmission. *Rootes Motors*

Right: Barreiros, which made trucks and buses, became Chrysler Espana S.A. in 1970 and was sold to Peugeot (PSA) in 1980, becoming part of Automoviles Talbot S.A. The 38-ton Barreiros tractor was marketed in Britain from 1973-77. After Rootes became Chrysler United Kingdom Ltd, it was known as the Dodge K3820P with 270bhp turbocharged 11.9-litre engine, replaced by the 300 Series. This 1974 tractor in the fleet of Sheffield's Frank Phillips (Haulage) Ltd is coupled to a two-axle flatbed platform trailer, with 'NORWAY ONLY' written on it. *Ian Allan Library*

Right: The 1974-registered Commer Commando was intended to replace the C and V Series and, eventually, the Dodge 500 K Series. It was also sold as a Dodge and (overseas) as a Fargo and De Soto. It is believed that this shot of the top of the 100 Series dates back to at least 1976. The Commando G1811P had a gcw of 18 tons and a 100in wheelbase. It had the new, improved Hi-Line tilt cab, the Perkins T6.354 engine and five-speed gearbox and Davies Magnet TJ3C fifth wheel; a two-speed Eaton rear axle was optional. In September 1977, the Dodge 20-ton G2011P tractor effectively replaced the 500K 20 and 22-ton K2011P and K2211P tractors. *Chrysler UK*

Right: The Dodge B300 Tradesman was adopted from April 1979 as the Dunstable-built 50 Series, and ran to March 1993. Initially the S35 (3.5 tonnes gross), S46 (4.5t), S56 (5.5t) and S66 (6.6t) were joined by an S75 (7.5t) in 1980, with chassis, chassis-cab and swb/lwb vans. Perkins 4.236, 6.247 and Chrysler 3.7-litre six-cylinder petrol models were available (though the latter was not in the S75), plus two-litre petrol on S35/46, with four or five-speed gearboxes. Severn Trent Water's S66V lwb, new in 1980/81, had an extended crew cab and tipper body. *Ian Allan Library*

Right: From 1 January 1979, PSA (Peugeot-Citroën) took over Chrysler's European operations. One year later, all three companies' names changed to 'Talbot' (e.g. Talbot Motor Co Ltd in the UK, Automoviles Talbot SA in Spain). The (re-)badging of cars was completed by 1981, save for the Dodge (Simca) half-ton van sold by Talbot car dealers. In January 1981, Renault Truck Industries Ltd and PSA combined to create Karrier Motors Ltd, whereupon the Renault diamond badge was added to 'Dodge' on the grilles. This July 1980 shot is of a new 24ft G1611 16-tonner, one of four for the well-known Wincanton vehicle and contract hire division. The sides and support posts could be completely removed in minutes. *Ian Allan Library*

Below: The Commando 2 was redesigned by Ogle and launched in 1981. By the end of 1983, the 6x4 24-ton G 24C was available, joining eight to 16-tonne 4x2 rigids and three tractor units. Karrier Motors became Renault Truck Industries Ltd that same year and, in 1984, the first Renault, the G260, was built in Dunstable.

The Commando 2 was then sold alongside the Renault R310 and R310 Turboliner. The 1987 facelift was the last (Renault-badged) Commando. New in October 1984, this Cheshire Highways Commando 2 G10 had an Edbro tipping body and was one of seven, with a Perkins 6.354 engine. *Perkins Engines*

DOUGLAS

F. L. Douglas (Equipment) Ltd was set up in 1947 in Cheltenham. It made its name with 4x4 short-wheelbase Transporter timber tractors, based on the AEC Matador – originally reconstructed ex-military vehicles, by 1954 they were made from new parts including the AEC Mk III cab. Other all-wheel-drive vehicles were added to the range, based on forward and normal control Commers, the Leyland Comet and other four and six-wheeled vehicles. The Pathfinder, a 1½-ton 4x4 based on a normal control Commer, was unfortunately a stillborn project.

Over the years, there has been a wide range of capacities available with two or four-wheel drive. Terminal tractors with an elevating fifth wheel were introduced (and are still produced today), including half-cab models with dual controls, along with various dump trucks which were less successful. The Tugmaster aircraft-towing tractor was also introduced.

In 1989, the company introduced its Douglas-Kalmar range of new technology including towbar-less aircraft-handling tractors. It has now become the world's foremost manufacturer of these units, in operation throughout Europe, Scandinavia, North America, the Middle East, Africa, Southeast Asia and the Far East.

Douglas has become one of the world's leading suppliers of aviation-towing tractors, ground support vehicles, port tractors, distribution and yard-shunting tractors. It has been manufacturing specialist airport, aircraft and military equipment for many years, with equipment in use in over 85 countries around the world.

Today, Douglas Equipment produces Douglas Tugmaster Towbarless and Conventional aircraft pushback and towing tractors, with low profiles, the option of elevated cabs and 'crab-steering'. The DC and TBL Series have capacities up to 600 tonnes, as well as Ro-Ro Terminal and Distribution tractors, and Mu-Meter equipment for measuring runway friction.

In April 2011, the former Douglas Equipment and Douglas SPD were acquired by INDAL Technologies, a business unit of Curtiss-Wright Flow Control Co with headquarters in Mississauga, Ontario, Canada.

Left: In the early post-World War 2 years, Douglas made its name by rebuilding ex-military AEC Matadors into timber tractors, then went on to build new vehicles using AEC parts. Many of these saw long, active lives and survive in semi-preservation.
Mike Forbes

Right: This tug was destined for oilfield duties. Similar vehicles were supplied as aircraft tugs for military and civilian applications in the 1950s. *CHC aan486*

Below: This Tugmaster was one of two used for loading and unloading trailers on Ro-Ro ships by East Coast Terminals & Storage Ltd at Immingham Docks. In this shot the ship is the Tor Anglia, registered in Gothenburg, Sweden. *PM Photography*

ERF

Edwin Richard Foden retired from the board of the Foden family concern in 1932, at the age of 62, after disagreements over the future of building steam lorries. His son Dennis and others persuaded him to put his faith in diesel-engined lorries into practice, forming the new company that bore his initials. From the start of production at Sandbach, Cheshire in 1933, ERF used proprietary components – which, at that time, meant Gardner engines and Jennings cabs.

The first vehicle, chassis No 63 (to mark Foden's age and give the impression that a number of chassis had already been built), was a 6-ton payload vehicle designated CI.4 (for Compression Ignition four-cylinder). The same basic design – designated CI.5 and CI.6 when powered by Gardner's 5LW and 6LW engines – remained in production until 1948. ERF also built 6-ton 4x2 military lorries during World War 2.

In 1948, a new range appeared with a curved radiator grille and a V-shaped windscreen, joined in 1951 by the Willenhall all-steel cab with its distinctively-shaped

front wings, also used by BMC, However, a much greater development occurred in November 1953, with the launch of the KV or 'Kleer Vue' cab. The new design – by Gerald Broadbent, who later came up with the Tautliner at Boalloy – took advantage of new glazing techniques to incorporate wraparound windscreens and a much more rounded cab. It also had an oval radiator grille that had been introduced on the previous cab design, earlier that same year.

Like their predecessors, most KVs were built on forward control chassis, some with a set-back front axle, but a semi-bonneted version was developed in the late 1950s to offer a three-man cab for the brewery trade, nicknamed Sabrina after a voluptuous starlet of the day. During this period, ERF began to broaden its range of engines, Gardner being complemented by Cummins and Rolls-Royce.

Right: ERF Ltd introduced a new range of lorries in 1948, with concealed radiators and V-shaped windscreens. This official shot of a Model 68 eight-wheeled flatbed platform rigid dates from August 1948. Apparently, a similar model was exhibited at the first post-war Commercial Motor Show that same year. *ERF*

Left: Burton-on-Trent, Staffordshire brewers Ind Coope and Samuel Allsopp merged in 1934 to form Ind Coope & Allsopp Ltd; later, in 1961, this merged with Ansells and Tetley Walker in 1961 to form Allied Breweries. This photograph of Ind Coope & Allsopp's six-wheeled brewer's dray, No 978, is dated September 1950. *ERF*

The KV was replaced in 1962 by the LV, a glass fibre-panelled cab with a single-piece curved windscreen. The following year saw ERF acquire Jennings, its main cab supplier since it began production. Around the same time, ERF also produced its first 32-ton truck. In 1970, the LV cab was revamped for the launch of a new chassis range: the A Series.

ERF had begun producing fire appliances in 1968, using a high-visibility cab developed by young freelance designer Ken Skelton. From 1977, this part of the business traded as Cheshire Fire Engineering, working from a separate site at Winsford. It was not a long-term success, however, and it closed in 1981.

In 1974, the A Series gave way to the B Series, with a similar chassis but an all-new steel-framed cab with sheet-moulded compound panels, the SP (Steel Plastic), also designed by Skelton. The A Series was not dropped completely until fullscale B Series production began in mid-1975. For some time ERF also fitted the steel Motor Panels cabs on export chassis, known as the MV, which was offered as an alternative for UK customers from 1972.

At the 1978 Motor Show, ERF showed the prototype of its M Series, a four-wheeled mediumweight 16-tonne gross model, with a lowered SP cab and Gardner 6LXB engine. This model also came with the option of a Dorman engine, both versions matched with a David Brown gearbox. Production of this new model, which extended ERF's range into the much larger market for lighter weight vehicles, was to be at a new site at Gresford, across the border in North Wales. However, an economic recession hit demand for new vehicles and the factory plan was shelved. It went into small-scale production at Sandbach and was re-launched in 1983 as the M16, but had a Perkins T6.354.4 engine in place of the Dorman.

The B Series was replaced by the C Series from 1981, and in 1985 the company introduced a CP (common parts) programme that offered a standard driveline of Cummins engine, Rockwell rear axle and Eaton gearbox. The company continued to offer other engines, gearboxes and axles, but its main emphasis was on the standard products and the Gardner option was finally dropped in 1990.

In 1986, the C Series gave way to the E Series, fitted with an updated version of the SP cab. (There was no D Series, as Ford has produced a model with that designation for 20 years and ERF wanted to avoid confusion.) To provide a stronger competitor against trucks imported from mainland Europe, the new EC

Top: This model 44G platform rigid was designed for 8 to 10-ton loads. In this October 1952 shot, it is seen in service with millers Mellor Mineral Mills Ltd of Etruria Vale, Stoke-on-Trent. Note the oval grille on the 1948 cab design, added from 1952. *Ian Allan Library*

Above: In November 1953, the KV ('Kleer-Vue') cab designed by Gerald Broadbent of Bowyer Bros was introduced. It had the oval grille, but with wraparound windscreens and a much more rounded outline. Photographed on 14 November 1953, Model 44G platform rigid No 91 was operated by William McEwan & Co Ltd of Fountain Brewery, Edinburgh, which had merged in 1931 with William Youngers of Edinburgh to form Scottish Brewers. In 1960, Scottish & Newcastle was created by a further merger with Newcastle Breweries. *ERF*

(European Community) appeared in 1993, in turn superseded by the ECX in 2000. Although these models were still fitted with SP cabs, ERF Plastics, the company that made the sheet-moulded compound panels, had been sold in 1990 to a Dutch company.

Although the M Series gained ERF a small share of the lighter truck market, the company made several attempts to offer a more widely acceptable model. In 1983, it signed a letter of intent to cooperate with Japanese manufacturer Hino on a 10 to 15-tonne model. This would have been assembled in Britain, with ERF supplying Eaton gearboxes and Cummins or Perkins engines matched to chassis, cabs and axles supplied by Hino. However, the project failed to proceed beyond the building of a prototype and, instead, a deal was struck later with (then) independent Austrian manufacturer Steyr to fit its perceptibly smaller all-steel cab onto the two- and three-axle Cummins-powered E Series models from 1988. These were known as the ES (E Steel), comprising the ES6 with Cummins B Series engine and ES8 with eight-litre C Series. The arrangement continued after Steyr was taken over by German manufacturer MAN in 1990.

In 1998, ERF introduced its 17-tonne EP6. Although badged as an ERF and fitted with the familiar driveline of Cummins B Series engine, Eaton gearbox and Meritor (formerly Rockwell) rear axle, it was less British than the stillborn Hino joint venture, having been built by the Turkish manufacturer BMC Sanayi (see BMC chapter). The arrangement suited both manufacturers, as ERF wanted to offer a cheaper light truck and BMC wanted to get into the UK market. The most distinctive feature of this rarely seen model is its cab, designed by Italian styling house Pininfarina. However, only a few were built before ERF started assembly of Isuzu light trucks on a contractual basis, after new owner PACCAR terminated Leyland's assembly contract with the Japanese manufacturer.

The EP6 may well owe its rarity to two changes in the ownership of ERF. Although listed on the London Stock Exchange since 1953, control of the company had remained with the family – principally E. R. Foden's youngest son, Peter, who was also managing

Right: The subsequent semi-forward control version of the KV cab, ostensibly for the brewery trade, was nicknamed the 'Sabrina' after voluptuous 1950s glamour model and actress Norma Sykes (aka Sabrina). This six-wheeled platform rigid was photographed in September 1958. *Ian Allan Library*

director. However, this last British-owned volume truck manufacturer ultimately bowed towards globalisation when it was taken over in 1996. The new owner was Western Star, a Canadian manufacturer of roughly equal size to ERF, owned by an Australian. As a North American manufacturer, Western Star also built trucks from bought-in components. However, this was only an interim phase, as the German manufacturer MAN bought ERF in early 2000, while Western Star took over the MAN import concession in Australia and New Zealand.

In August 1999 it was announced that ERF production was to be transferred from Sandbach to nearby Middlewich, where a new factory opened in

Pochin Way during 2000. In March 2000, Canadian truck manufacturer Western Star completed the sale of its subsidiary ERF (Sandbach Engineering Ltd) to MAN, the new company becoming MAN-ERF Ltd. The takeover quickly resulted in a new ECS range of vehicles with the MAN F2000 steel cab and ECX with GRP cab. In the longer term, it was expected that MAN's lower weight trucks would be badged as ERFs and sold through the UK dealer network. As with the short-lived, Turkish-built EP6, with its Steyr cabs, these would be MAN lorries with ERF badges. In addition, the ES6 and ES8 range continued in the new plant, having transferred from the old Middlewich ERF Service Centre. They used Cummins six-litre B and eight-litre

Left: By 1960, the KV cab was updated with twin headlamps while certain models featured a set-back front axle for improved weight distribution. This shot is dated March 1963 and shows a new eight-wheel model 88R with a 4,000-gallon alloy fuel-oil tank, operated by Saddler & Co (Transport) Ltd of Middlesbrough on behalf of Total Oil Products (GB) Ltd. *ERF*

C Series power units in ERF running gear with the Steyr Cab, which would become the MAN L2000 cab after Steyr was taken over by MAN. Once the ECL and ECM vehicles became available, the ES6 and 8 were inevitably dropped.

Middlewich produced 2,800 vehicles in 2001 and MAN intended to increase assembly to 3,000 per year. However, in August 2001, accounting irregularities were found and the resultant problems at its subsidiary gave MAN the opportunity to restructure British operations, 'integrating' the product range. Production ended at Middlewich in July 2002 and about 200 employees were made redundant, al though about 50 were retained to adapt Munich-built vehicles (see below) for specific customer needs.

In April 2005, MAN-ERF Ltd was awarded an order for just under 5,200 trucks by the Ministry of Defence, which was worth 1.5 billion euros and provided an option for approximately 2,100 more vehicles, Delivery started in 2007 and should finish in 2013.

From 2000, ERF's final model range also included the ECT, ECM and ECL models, which were built on MAN's production line in Nuremburg. However, after Middlewich closed (as announced on 11 September 2001), ECT, ECM and ECL model production moved to Munich and ECT to Saltzgitter, Germany. In early production, the German-built ERF ECT was a Cummins ISM-powered TG-A with grille and badge change, though a handful of MAN D28-powered vehicles was also built, which eventually outnumbered the Cummins-powered units. The ECL (ERF-badged MAN L2000 with MAN D08 engine) and ECM (ERF-badged MAN M2000, some with Cummins

Left: In 1962, the KV cab was replaced by its LV GRP counterpart, which had a single-piece curved windscreen. This is an early version built by Boalloy, as seen from the vertical door handles. The main power units were the Gardner 150 and 180 engines. The former was fitted in this new eight-wheeled dropside, photographed in January 1963 when in service with Aberdare Cables Ltd, evidently provided on test by the Sandbach plant. *ERF*

Left: A. & H. Davey (Roadways) Ltd of Stoke-on-Trent acquired two model 68GX eight-wheelers with 150bhp Gardner 6LX engines in January 1965. Both had coil-carrying bodies and cabs with conventional door handles by coachbuilders J. H. Jennings of Sandbach, acquired in 1963 by ERF, its main cab supplier from the start of production. These vehicles were among the first to have the new-style name on the radiator grille. *ERF*

Right: This summer of 1966-registered Cummins-engined tractor (No 11) was the first in service with Channel Road Services, coupled to a York TIR van trailer for use on Continental 'smalls' traffic. Note the three air-vent grilles above the grille badge. *Ian Allan Library*

Left: This new 1970 model 64CU180 has the 180bhp Cummins NHE engine with a David Brown six-speed gearbox, BDR rear axle and full air spring braking system. It has a revised cab with additional air-vent grilles above the number plate. The 25-ton BTC 20ft low-loader has a 6½-ton winch and two heavy duty hydraulic jacks. F. T. Seagrim & Co Ltd of Cheltenham was a heavy haulier and transported the plant equipment. *Ian Allan Library*

ISBe and some with MAN D08 engine) models were shipped to the UK and modified for UK operation in the Middlewich VMU (Vehicle Modification Unit) by a handful of old ERF production workers. (Their main work at this point was firescreens, as tanker fleets were the only significant gain MAN had made via the old ERF customer base.) The VMU closed in 2006/7 after final job losses, apart from a few who transferred to Beech's Garage at Stoke to carry on modification work.

In the light of Cummins' apparent delay in upgrading the ISMe engine to comply with Euro4 emission regulations, MAN took the initial decision to replace it completely in the ECT range with the new series of MAN D20 engines. However, with ERF badging used only for the British market, MAN decided to cease the supply of ERF-badged trucks from July 2007. MAN-ERF UK Ltd then changed its name to MAN Truck & Bus UK Ltd and, in 2008, closed its training school.

Above: ERF introduced the new A Series in 1972. There was a new range of tractor units and 28 to 30-ton gvw 8x2 tippers to meet new regulations governing four-axle rigid operations. This 1972-registered 180bhp Gardner-engined 30-ton model 68GXB (with revised LV cab) had a Dyson body and was used to haul bulk fuel. *ERF*

Left: The 34-tonne gcw tractor unit was offered with either a six-cylinder Cummins or a six or eight-cylinder Gardner engine. A 38-tonne European version was also built, with a tilting cab. This model LAC 340 had the Cummins NH 225 engine and was photographed before display at the 1973 Scottish Motor Show. By 1975, there was also a 36-tonne (design weight) model LAC 360 with Cummins NHC 250 engine. *ERF*

Right: This shot dates from May 1973 and shows a 32-ton gcw A Series Cummins-engined model MCC 340, with the ERF continental-type all-steel Motor Panels sleeper cab (as specified by operators Beresford Transport of Stoke-on-Trent, for weekly services to Basle and internal Swiss distribution). Beresford purchased 14 Cummins and Gardner-engined tractors, all with twin 50-gallon fuel tanks and automatic lubrication, for use with Peak three-axle 2950 cu ft Super-cube trailers. *Ian Allan Library*

Below: The B Series was introduced in September 1974 with a shared SP cab using hot press-moulded GRP panels over a steel frame, offered with Gardner, Cummins and Rolls-Royce power units. This 1975-registered model 31G4 four-axle rigid, with a 180bhp Gardner engine (the 150bhp was also available) and tipper body, was in the fleet of Wherry & Sons Ltd of Bourne, Lincolnshire. The tractors had York fifth wheels and were available up to 38 tons gross. *Ian Allan Library*

Above: This tractor was new in 1980/81 and had a Jennings sleeper-cab conversion, Gardner 8LXB engine, Fuller gearbox and Eaton rear axle. It was in service with R. J. & I. Monkhouse of Brampton, near Carlisle, and carried 50ft lengths of steel. Limited to 32.5 tonnes gross at first, after the 1983 Armitage Report it was able to run at 38 tonnes with a tri-axle trailer. *Ian Allan Library*

Left: The C Series replaced the B Series in late 1981, with similar engine options. The 50,000th ERF was handed over by Peter Foden in 1984 to the Mobil Oil Co, one of its longest-standing customers, completing an order for 14 vehicles. Chassis 50,063 (numbering started with 63 – the first ERF, as can also be seen in the picture) was designated 32C2, plated at 32 tonnes, with the SP3 cab, Cummins L10 250 243bhp turbocharged engine, Spicer 10-speed gearbox and Rockwell axle. The day cab was constructed by ERF's SMC operation, and fire-screened for use with petroleum spirit. In 1984, the designation badge was dropped from the cab doors and the CP range was launched. All had Cummins engines and were 4x2, 6x2 or 6x4 drive, with a choice of day or sleeper cabs. *Ian Allan Library*

Right: There was no D Series (to avoid confusion with the Ford D Series) and so ERF introduced the E Series in 1986, with an updated SP cab. This was available with Cummins, Rolls-Royce (later owned by Perkins) or Gardner engines in the E16 range until the late 1980s. The ERF logo was relocated to the upper left of the grille and a badge denoting engine size was placed on the lower right of the grille. H. Tidewell & Sons Ltd's six-wheeled (four-wheeled also available) E14, as seen here, carried a 1987/8 registration and a sleeper cab.
PM Photography

Left: To provide stronger competition against trucks imported from mainland Europe, the new EC range appeared in 1993. This was the last true ERF design prior to its being taken over by Western Star. These two EC12 eight-wheeled tippers were in service with Yuill & Dodds of Strathaven Scotland, numbered 23 (registered 1992/3) and 35 (1994/5).
PM Photography

Above: Western Star sold out to MAN of Germany in 2000. The takeover quickly resulted in the appearance of a new Middlewich-assembled ECS range of lorries, carrying the MAN F2000 steel cab and ECX range with GRP cab. This 2001 ECX six-wheeled tractor was No 78 in Wm Morrison's supermarket fleet. *PM Photography*

Left: An example of a German-built ERF from 2004/5, effectively the same as a MAN, delivered near the end of production for these 'badge-engineered' vehicles in 2007. *PM Photography*

FODEN

Edwin Foden designed his first steam tractor in 1882, making efficient use of a compound engine, and it came into regular production from about 1887. Within 10 years, load-carrying steam lorries would be on the market and, in 1902, production of the well-known Foden 5-ton lorry commenced, running until 1923. The superior performance of the petrol (later oil) engine, plus heavy taxation and legislation affecting steam vehicles, sounded the latters' death knell. From 1931, the Sandbach, Cheshire-based company turned its attention to diesel-powered lorries using Gardner (and later several other makes of) oil engines.

In the eight years up to the outbreak of World War 2, the company produced a large number of commercial vehicles, ranging from 4-ton to 15-ton payloads, all featuring the same distinctive but conventional design of radiator grille. During the war, the company supplied 6x4 army lorries and parts for Centaur and Crusader tanks, as well as munitions of various types.

Civilian production recommenced soon after the cessation of hostilities, the pre-war types now using a new cab design known as the DG, modernised with a curved front, and the radiator grille blending into the new outline. This was updated as the FG or FE, depending on whether a Gardner diesel or the revolutionary Foden FD6 two-stroke diesel engine (produced until 1977) was used. The new S18 cab was designed for this model.

The Steel Company of Wales had first placed an order in 1946 for a large capacity tipper, the first of many giant dumptrucks to be manufactured over the years. This particular model looks small today, but at the time it was regarded as huge.

Further modernisation took place by 1956, when power-assisted steering was introduced along with the S20 cab, still a traditional coachbuilt structure with metal panels on wooden frames and fitted to many Foden lorries until at least 1963. However, 1958 saw the introduction of lightweight glass-reinforced plastic (GRP) for cab production, with the first Foden GRP cab, the distinctively-styled S21 model, nicknamed the 'Mickey Mouse' or 'Sputnik' because of the unusual shape of the windscreens. The first British-built, mass-produced tilting cab, designated the S24, followed in

Left: After World War 2, Foden Ltd initially reintroduced its old models with few improvements, though the company also entered the bus chassis market in 1946. The completely new FE and FG lorry ranges were introduced in 1948, along with the new Foden FD6 two-stroke diesel engine. This August 1949 photograph of a six-wheeled FG heavy tipper appears to have been taken outside the Sandbach works, with newly built lorries in the background. It was No 124 on the fleet of Edmund Nuttall & Sons (London) Ltd. Note the cross-country bar-tread tyres on the rear axles.
Ian Allan Library

Left: Crossing Tower Bridge in Central London in 1950, this nearly new eight-wheeled platform lorry is either a Model S18 FE6/15 or the optional Gardner 6LW-engined S18 FG6/15, in the fleet of wire manufacturers Richard Johnson & Nephew Ltd of Ambergate, near Derby. *Ian Allan Library*

Foden family finally lost control of their long-established business. The new owner was PACCAR (truncated from its original name of Pacific Car), an ambitious family-owned company based at Seattle in the USA. PACCAR already owned the Kenworth and Peterbilt truck brands on its own side of the Atlantic and the Foden approach of building vehicles from proprietary components fitted well with American practice, with the new owner able to strip out many of the costs that had brought down the old company. PACCAR kept the Foden brand name for the Cheshire-built vehicles, but for a time the company traded as Sandbach Engineering before being renamed Foden Trucks.

Just before the takeover, Foden launched the S10 Series that comprised the S104 four-wheeled, S106 six-wheeled and S108 eight-wheeled models. These were redesignated as the 4000 Series in 1989, with exact numbers to denote the engine's power output (eg 4275 for the 275hp Cummins L10 version).

The S10 and 4000 Series were fitted with 2.5m-wide cabs, but a 2.2m version of the same glass-fibre cab was introduced from 1989, for customers looking for smaller, lighter vehicles. First of these new models was the 2000 Series 17-tonner with a Cummins or Perkins engine, followed in 1992 by the 3000, which offered a narrower cab on heavier trucks. Choice of engines across the range was expanded to include the Cummins B, C, L10, M11 and N14, or the Perkins Eagle and Caterpillar.

One further innovation from Foden around this time was a new fully electronic air suspension system for its twin-steer tractors, while the cab interiors were also completely redesigned. When the range was revamped in 1992, with a revised grille design, the distinctive kite-shaped Foden radiator badge was confined to the inside of a small round logo. This did not prove popular,

1962, designed to give complete unobstructed access to the engine and mechanical components (although S21 cab production still continued until 1969).

In 1964, a change in the Construction & Use Regulations favoured articulated vehicles over the older rigid designs and new models were introduced to compete in the 32-ton market. More than 75% of heavy chassis sold in Britain in the following years were tractor units. In 1968, a half-cab with forward-angled windscreens could be mounted low on the chassis as a special order for cranes or the carriage of long girders, but this also found its way onto some tippers, mixers and even a few tractor units.

A new factory was opened in 1974 due to increased production. Later, the company ran into financial difficulties, but a large NATO order offered recovery. New Fleetmaster and Haulmaster models, with steel tilt cabs manufactured by Motor Panels, were introduced in 1977. The Fleetmaster was normally fitted with a Cummins or Rolls-Royce 290bhp engine and the Haulmaster – which had a slightly different radiator grille and split windscreen – with a Cummins, Gardner or Rolls-Royce 180-265bhp engine. These models were also available from 1979 with a glass-fibre and aluminium cab.

The problems that followed the opening of the new factory came back to haunt Foden in 1980, when a deepening recession cut demand for new trucks by over 40%. This time the receivers were called in and the however, and the kite was soon restored to somewhere closer to its original prominent position.

Even bigger changes followed as a result of PACCAR's acquisition of DAF Trucks in 1996 and Leyland Trucks in 1998. A Dutch-born managing director was put in charge of Sandbach, and the S10-derived models were replaced by the Alpha which used the same steel cab structure as DAF's 85 Series.

This was symptomatic of a more fundamental change in the way Foden built and sold its trucks. Instead of building vehicles to order with a choice of engine transmission and axle options, the Alpha introduced a range of models for different market sectors. Standard engines were the Cummins B, C or M11, or the Caterpillar 3126 or C10, while transmissions were mainly Eaton or ZF. Axles were by Meritor. With the impending introduction of Euro 3 emissions standards in October 2001, Foden standardised on the Cummins ISBe and ISMe, and the Caterpillar 3126E and C12, engines.

Truck production at Sandbach finally ended in the spring of 2000, moving to the Leyland plant in Lancashire. The Foden brand was kept alive for a while, but a diminishing market forced a rundown. The last vehicles were built in 2006, coinciding with the Foden company's 150th anniversary.

Right: This four-wheeled OG4/6 on the fleet of the Winsford Industrial Co-operative Society, Cheshire was new in June 1951, although it looks much older with its exposed radiator. *Ian Allan Library*

Left: The 8-ton FE4/8 model was launched in 1953, with a supercharged four-cylinder two-stroke engine mounted underfloor. The cab was a three-man type, aluminium on a wooden frame. This demonstrator had an 18ft alloy platform body. *Ian Allan Library*

Left: This eight-wheeled Gardner-engined FG6/15 had a five-speed gearbox and a special tipping tanker body by Airscrew & Jigwood Ltd of London. When photographed in July 1954 it was British Sugar Corporation No 1, used for delivering bulk sugar.
Ian Allan Library

Right : Fodens produced a long line of earth-moving dumper trucks. This September 1954 shot is of a model 7ED6 with a two-stroke six-cylinder engine and eight-speed gearbox.
Ian Allan Library

Right: This model FGHT
8/80 heavy tractor, with its
special cab, was in service
in November 1957 with
the famous Sunter Bros
of Northallerton, Yorkshire.
Ian Allan Library

Left: This April 1957 shot is
of a FE/6-24 eight-wheeled
tanker, one of a large fleet
supplied to Murgatroyd's
Salt and Chemical Co Ltd of
Elworth, Sandbach, Cheshire.
It had a six-cylinder two-
stroke diesel engine and
five-speed super low gearbox,
double-drive rear bogie
axles and giant pneumatic
tyres, plus the metal-panels-
on-wooden frame S20 cab
introduced in 1956 and used
until 1963. *Ian Allan Library*

Above: This was the first Python aircraft refueller built for the Esso Petroleum Co Ltd by Thompson Bros (Bilston) Ltd. It was handed over at London Heathrow Airport on 22 September 1960.
Ian Allan Library

Right: This December 1960 view shows the all-GRP S21 (nicknamed the 'Mickey Mouse' or 'Sputnik' cab) with wrap-around screens, as offered from 1958-69. This eight-wheeled tipper was new to the city of Salford.
Ian Allan Library

Right: A three-axle dump truck with twin wheels on the rear axles. This shot was taken in June 1961. *Ian Allan Library*

Below: The S24, introduced in 1962, was the UK's first mass-produced tilt cab and was derived from the S21. This eight-wheeled chassis was presumably destined for the 1962 London Commercial Motor Show, as the photograph is dated September 1962.
Ian Allan Library

Left: This special low-cab eight-wheeler was new in 1965 to T. A. Bulmer & Co Ltd of Middlesbrough, for carrying lengths of steel girder. A similar design was fitted to crane carriers. *Ian Allan Library*

Left: This tractor unit with S40 cab plus reversed-sloping screen (also available as a half-cab) was registered in August 1970 and appears to be a demonstrator for the then new Crane Fruehauf Continental TIR trailer. *Ian Allan Library*

Left: This artic tractor unit, seen with a step-frame high-cube trailer, has the roomy S80 cab with large headlights, as fitted to most Foden models during the early 1970s. *Ian Allan Library*

Above: The Fleetmaster that became available by 1977 was offered with lhd or rhd, day or sleeper cabs, and used a full-screen version of the S95 all-steel cab. Engines were 290bhp Cummins or Rolls-Royce 290L with Fuller gearboxes, Lipe Rollway clutch and Rockwell hypoid rear axle. Heygates of Northampton's No 143 is seen coupled to a flour tanker built by Carmichael of Worcester. *Foden*

Right: This 1979 Gardner 6LXC-engined eight-wheeled S10 Haulmaster tipper, in service with Griffith, had an eight-speed gearbox. *Ian Allan Library*

Left: This six-wheeled tipper is the heavy-duty RC29/26 Superhaulmaster, with the Cummins engine option.
Ian Allan Library

Below: This 1993 Foden 4380 three-axle tractor unit shows how the S10-derived 4000 Series cab had only a small Foden 'kite' badge at the time.
PM Photography

Right: After the takeover of Leyland Trucks by PACCAR in 1998, independent Foden production ceased. It was replaced by Leyland-built models which used cabs from DAF, also acquired by PACCAR in 1996, which had the option of CAT, Detroit Diesel or Cummins ISMe engines. This 2001/2 Alpha 3000 eight-wheeled tipper was operated by John B. L. Gill & Son. *PM Photography*

Below: In 2005, it was announced by PACCAR that Foden production was likely to cease in the next year, to release manufacturing capacity at Leyland Trucks for increased volume of the DAF brand. This 2005 six-wheeled tractor was No 268 in Wm Morrison's supermarket fleet, having been supplied about a year before the last Foden was built in 2006. *PM Photography*

FORD / IVECO-FORD *including* FORDSON & THAMES

1908-97

Ford began to export its cars to England in 1904, followed four years later by the Model T lorry. From 1911, however, assembly of the latter began at the company's premises at Trafford Park, Manchester. The Ford Model T continued until 1927, when the Model A was introduced. The company's move to Dagenham, Essex, was effected in 1931, and from then onwards the vehicles were (more or less) of English design and manufacture.

The Ford contribution to the war effort was immense, making Bren Gun Carriers and other half-tracked vehicles, general service 15-cwt trucks and 4x4 forward control three-tonners for the Army and other services. It also produced six-wheeled winch lorries for barrage balloons, mobile canteens and fire tenders.

The name 'Fordson' had been adopted for commercial vehicles from about 1929; in late 1939, the word 'Thames' was introduced as a local reference. After the war, the forward control Fordson 7V, with its V8 petrol engine, continued in production until the normal control ET6, with the same petrol engine, or ET7, with a Perkins

diesel, replaced it in 1950. From 1954, the choice of a four-cylinder petrol or Ford's own diesel engine became available in the ET6, known as the 'Cost Cutter'.

In 1957, the semi-forward control Thames (not Fordson) Trader was introduced – its variations offering payloads from 30-cwt to 7 tons, with four or six-cylinder petrol or diesel engines – and continued for the next

Below: The first Fordson lorries were built at the Dagenham Plant in 1934. From 1937, the forward control Fordson 7V model was badged as 'Fordson Thames', and was built throughout the war for the Ministry of Supply and other essential uses. Until 1946, it was available as a hydraulic tipper, a 143½in-wheelbase lorry, a van, a County Commercial Cars-converted 6x2 and 6x4 chassis, and a 118in-wheelbase truck. Production restarted for the commercial markets in the 2 to 5-ton payload range, until replaced in 1949. The late 1946-registered 7V seen here had a baker's van body applied to its 143½in wheelbase chassis for Coombe Bakery of Teddington by Lamberts of Kingston Ltd. Note the twin rear wheels. *Ford*

Left: The Fordson Thames ET6 and ET7 were launched as normal control trucks in 1949. The ET6 was powered by the V8 L-head or, from 1954, four-cylinder petrol engines, while the ET7 had a Perkins P6 diesel engine. The new models covered a range similar to the 7V, including the County six-wheeled conversions. This Ford-owned ET6 dropside lorry has the four-cylinder Cost Cutter petrol engine and was registered in spring 1953. *Ford*

Below: By 1955, the 4D version of the Thames ET6 had been fitted with a four-cylinder diesel engine similar to that of the Fordson E1A Major tractor. This 1956 shot is of a 1955-registered 3-ton 4D, No 121 in the fleet of East London builders' merchants Nicholls & Clarke Ltd. The cabs were built by Briggs Motor Bodies Ltd of Dagenham, Southampton and Doncaster, similar to those used by Dodge, Leyland and Guy. Ford had acquired Briggs in 1953. *Ian Allan Library*

range was redesigned in 1978 and continued in production until 1981, when the new Cargo range was announced. The smaller Ford A Series, which was never as successful, was introduced in the early 1970s and ceased production in 1983.

eight years. A Mk II version appeared in 1962. The bonneted Thames Trader K Series was introduced at this time, with a range from 2-8 tons, some models being available with several different wheelbases. The K Series remained in production until 1972.

The forward control Thames 400E Series 10/12 and 15-cwt made its appearance at the same time as the Trader. This was the forerunner of the highly successful Transit van, which was produced from August 1965, and initial assembly was at Langley, near Slough, Berkshire, before moving to Swaythling, Southampton, in 1972.

The Langley-built D Series forward control vehicles also made their appearance in 1965, catering for loads from 5-28 tons, including tractor units for use with semi-trailers in several different weight ranges. The

Ford's first venture into the 'heavy duty' market was the H Series Transcontinental range (32-44 tons) introduced in 1975. This was not really a British vehicle, as the engine came from Cummins, the gearbox from Fuller, the axles from Rockwell, the cab assembly from Berliet (later absorbed by Renault) and the whole collection was assembled in Amsterdam. In 1982, when the Amsterdam plant closed, the final assembly was undertaken at Sandbach Engineering (Foden) while the cabs were painted at the Karrier factory in Dunstable. These vehicles never enjoyed great success, as they faced considerable competition from other foreign manufacturers, and the range was discontinued in 1983.

In July 1986, Iveco (Industrial Vehicles Corporation), the commercial vehicle wing of Fiat (into which OM,

Left: The ET6/ET7 models were replaced in 1957 by the Thames Trader semi-forward control range, covering weights from 2-7 tons and powered by either four or six-cylinder petrol engines, or 4D and 6D four and six-cylinder diesel engines, with four-cylinder engines up to 3 tons and six cylinders above this weight – as indicated by the red-painted '4', '6', '4D' or '6D' in a chrome badge on the front wing. The lighter weight vehicles were available with 118in and 138in wheelbases, the heavyweight vehicles with 138in, 152in and 160in wheelbases. Additionally, there was a 108in-wheelbase tipper chassis, for which 4x4 conversions were offered, and also a low-frame chassis model. This diesel-engined Trader was registered in 1958; it is seen on Armistice Day in 1961, carrying two empty drums for the fleet of British Ropes Ltd. *Ian Allan Library*

Unic and Magrius-Deutz had already been absorbed), took control of all the Ford commercial vehicles over 3.5 tonnes. From that time onwards, the products were badged as 'Iveco'.

The Ford Cargo models superseded the D Series in 1981. The range extended from 6-38 tonnes, including tractor units, all with a choice of wheelbase and predominantly fitted with Cummins, Perkins or Deutz engines. The series can easily be distinguished by its deep quarter lights at the side of the cabs. The Cargo range was also merged with Iveco when the changeover was made.

Ford's greatest success has been the Transit van, from the time that the first model was introduced in 1965. The Transit was completely redesigned in 1986, with a new aerodynamic front end. Models are now produced for loads from 750 kg to 3.5 tonnes, and altogether the Transit is available in three different wheelbases, five body styles, seven different payloads and four engine options. Ford has also continued with light vans based on its car chassis and engines. The Transit has been revamped several times and will remain in in production at Southampton until 2013 – though in future the model will be restricted to chassis cabs only, vans being built in Turkey.

Between 1991-3, the entire Iveco truck range was replaced by a new integrated range from 6-44 tonnes, with a steel/plastic cab by the Ital Design styling team in Italy. These vehicles were built at all of Iveco's assembly plants, in Italy, Germany, Spain and the UK. They were significant for Britain in that they replaced the 1981 Cargo design – the last Ford-developed product – although production of this model was transferred to the Indian manufacturer Ashok Leyland, in which Iveco had a significant financial stake.

The Cargo's replacement was sold in mainland Europe as the EuroCargo (other models in the range had names like EuroTech and EuroTrakker), but initially known in the UK as New Cargo. This 6 to 34-tonne range was powered initially by Iveco engines and began with models produced at Langley, where the Ford-designed Cargo had been built. However, this was a short-lived arrangement. Although Iveco had been in control of the Iveco Ford Truck joint venture from 1986, Ford still had an interest in the venture and owned the Langley site. Partly in order to realise the value of this asset on a key trunk road leading into London and to nearby Heathrow Airport, Ford closed the Langley plant in 1977 for redevelopment. Production of the Cargo was transferred to Italy, where the Iveco truck range continues to be built.

Right: The Langley, Buckinghamshire Truck Plant is believed to have started production in 1959, using cabs supplied by the former Briggs plant in Southampton. These four petrol-engined Trader Luton vans, photographed in 1961, were built there. They were Nos. 61-64 in the fleet of Benjamin Electric Ltd of Tottenham, North London, and had a ulw of 5 tons. *Ian Allan Library*

Above: County Commercial Cars Ltd of Fleet, Hampshire, continued to supply 6x2 and 6x4 conversions for installation on the production line, though other six-wheel (including 6x6) and 4x4 conversions were offered by other companies. This 6D-engined County 6x4 has a 137in-wheelbase chassis, five-speed David Brown gearbox and 5 cu yd truck-mixer. *Ian Allan Library*

Left: The Trader was available as a tractor unit. This 1962 6D-engined vehicle is coupled to a chassis-less aluminium construction van trailer by the British Trailer Co Ltd and Alcan Industries Ltd with 'four-in-line' suspension.
Alcan Industries

Below: The Trader Mk II was introduced in mid-1962. It had different badging, with the word 'TRADER' in white letters spaced out between the headlights, replacing the divider and badge. The diesel-engined models had '4D' or '6D' chrome badges on each front wing. The lower edge of the badge had a horizontal chrome strip running the length of the lower part of the wing.

Payloads were up to 7½ tons, with a 17-ton gross tractor unit. Six-wheeled County (and other companies') conversions were also offered again. This 1963-registered 6D-engined Mk 2 was No 243 with the fleet of I. Leftley Ltd of Barking, Essex.
Ian Allan Library

Right: The normal control Thames Trader (620E series) was introduced in 1962, alongside the Mk II forward control. The cab was built by Pressed Steel, rather than at the Southampton plant, and was based on the German Ford Köln KV. Four-cylinder petrol and diesel engines were offered. The models were 15, with 132in wheelbase and single rear wheels, duals on the 20 (132-146in wheelbase), 30 and 40 (both 146-166in wheelbase). Single or two-speed axles were available. The K series or 640E, originated in April 1965, used the same cab and continued until 1972. This new 40 dropside has the 4D engine.
Ian Allan Library

Above: The Langley-built Ford D series was a range of middleweight trucks introduced in April 1965. The initial range covered rigid trucks with gross weights from 5.2-12.75 tons, and tippers from 10.8-12.75 tons. Higher gross weights and articulated versions were quickly added to the range. This early 1965 shot shows a D series tractor, which may have been a pre-series production unit. It is coupled to a Boden semi-trailer carrying eight Southampton-built cabs. Three new diesel engines were developed for the trucks, of 3.97, 5.42 and 5.95 litres respectively. The smallest unit was of four cylinders while the larger engines employed six. Possibly with an eye to export markets outside Europe, petrol-engined versions with power outputs of 129bhp and 149bhp were also offered.
Ian Allan Library

Right: This 1966-registered D800 tipper was photographed on a housing site in May 1968. It had an Edbro twin-ram underbody assembly, lifting a body built by operator N. J. Grose Ltd of Holmbush, St Austell.
Ian Allan Library

Right: The D300 'Baby' artic, as it was known, was introduced by spring 1967. It had a plated gcw of 20,500lb, having been designed by the Ford Special Vehicle Order department and developed in conjunction with Hands (Letchworth) Ltd, a Hawker-Siddeley Group company. This 1967-registered unit was on the fleet of Bristow & Copley & Co Ltd of Longford, Coventry (then part of the Powell Duffryn group).
Hands Trailers

Below right: In April 1967, the range was extended by the arrival of the Phase II D1000 series, designed for operation up to a weight of 28 tons gross using Cummins 7.7-litre V8 diesel engines. In August 1968, Ford announced the new tandem-axle six-wheeled truck and tipper chassis, the DT1400 range, and the new Ford 150bhp 360 cu in turbocharged diesel. They were designed for 20-ton gvw operation with a body/payload allowance of 15 tons. The 6x2 version was for highway operation, the 6x4 for on/off-road use and, as here, the non-reactive two-spring 6x4 for more arduous off-road use. *Ford*

Left: This May 1973 shot is of a 226in wheelbase D2818 drawbar trailer, the eighth Ford acquired by London-based Vannic International. It had a well-appointed Steels Ltd two-berth sleeper cab conversion, complete with a stereo radio/tape player and Bostrom suspension seats, and a trailer by Crane Fruehauf. On TIR work it had a gtw of 28 tons and could carry stone or metal sculptures that weighed 10 tons or more. The engine was a 180bhp Cummins 504 V8, driven through an eight-speed gearbox. *Ford*

Left: The 1975-83 H Series Transcontinental range (32-44 tons) used Berliet cabs, a 14-litre Cummins engine with typical outputs of 290-350hp, Fuller and Eaton transmissions and Rockwell axles. When the Amsterdam plant closed in 1982, 504 more of them were built at the Foden Vehicle Assembly Plant in Sandbach. Seven 1975/6-registered Transcontinental tractors from the Brain Haulage fleet are seen lined up here in various contract liveries. *Ian Allan Library*

Left: The Ford A Series was built at Langley from 1972-84 to fill the gap between the heaviest Transit, at 3.5 metric tonnes gvw, and the 7-tonne D Series. The A Series cab shared most of its components with the Transit, but retained its profile for the entire period of production – it was never updated like the Transits. The smaller A04xx series had 14in wheels and four-cylinder engines; the bigger A05xx/ A06xx series had 16in wheels, a stronger frame and six-cylinder engines. This 1975/6-registered A0609 chassis-cab had a 2 cu yd capacity mixer unit and was owned by Mini Mix Concrete Ltd of Rainham, Essex. *Ford*

Above: This shot dates from 1979 and shows the updated D Series cab design. This D1614 chassis cab had a 226in wheelbase and a Ford six-litre turbo-diesel with six-speed gearbox and power take-off (PTO). The body was by Welford Truck Bodies Ltd, one of 70 (including Welford P666/6MMuscle Loaders) in the George Wimpey Ltd fleet. *Ian Allan Library*

Left: Seen here in a quarry in the summer of 1980, H&S Contractors' (Farningham) DT2418 tipper had a 169in wheelbase and tandem-drive bogie in four-spring configuration. It also had the 171PS 8.3-litre Cummins and Ford 8-570-S eight-speed range-change gearbox, 13 cu m steel tipper body by Hydro Hoist Ltd of New Addington and Edbro 5LNC front ram. *Ford*

Right: This non-HGV D0710 120in wheelbase chassis with custom cab had a Birchwood Ltd (of Erith, Kent) tipper body and a gvw of 748kg. The engine was the 100hp normally-aspirated Ford six-litre diesel driving through a Ford 6-600-S six-speed gearbox. *Ford*

Below: Introduced in 1981, the Langley-built Cargo replaced the D series and was deemed to be 'Truck of the Year 1982'. This view is of the production line, embargoed until 7 January 1982, showing chassis cabs that underwent major assemblies at plants in Dagenham, Swansea, Southampton and Enfield. *Ford*

Left: After the Amsterdam plant closed in 1982, 504 more units were assembled by the Foden VAP (Vehicle Assembly Plant) in Sandbach until 1983. This is a 1983-registered Transcontinental 4428 tractor, in the fleet of Star Transport (which, judging by the telephone number, was based in Kingston-upon-Hull). *PM Photography*

Below: As a consequence of Transcontinental tractors ceasing production, Ford introduced a new range of heavyweight Cargo tractor units ranging from 28-38 tonnes gcw. The 38-tonners were powered by the Cummins L10, while those at 28 and 32 tonnes had Perkins, Cummins or air-cooled Deutz diesel engines. This December 1982 view shows one of 17 Cargo 3220 32-tonne tractors with a 204bhp Deutz 9.6-litre air-cooled engine. It had 100-gallon fuel tanks and, surprisingly, heated mirrors. *Ian Allan Library*

Above: In August 1983, it was announced that a sleeper cab would be available on the Cargo chassis. This was a 16.25-tonne gross Cummins-engined 1617 operated by T&D Transport of Southsea, Hampshire. It was one of six validation units released to the UK before volume production commenced in October of that year and was supplied by Hendy Lennox (Cosham) Ltd, now known as Hendy Ford. Today the company still sells Ford commercials and IVECO vans and lorries (including Eurocargos). *Ford*

Above: This November 1983 view is of one of 38 Cargos for St Ivel (a subsidiary of Unigate dairies), ordered by Wincanton Transport (part of Wincanton Group, another Unigate subsidiary). They included fifteen 1011 10½-ton chassis, fifteen 1313 12½-ton chassis, as seen here, and eight 1615 16¼-ton chassis. The bodywork was built using GRP panels and ranged from 17½ft to 25ft on the 1615 chassis. *Ian Allan Library*

Left: This August 1985 shot shows two of the first six Cargo 3224 tractors to join the fleet of William West & Sons Ltd of Ilkeston, Nottinghamshire. They had a 243bhp Cummins L10-250 engine and were used for trunking operations for Boots PLC. They also ran at 32.5 tonnes gross and had Fuller-Eaton RT11609 gearboxes and Eaton 23000 Series rear axles, twin fuel tanks totalling 300 litres and a standard sleeper cab with an under-bumper air dam, and had the optional rear anti-roll bar, heavy duty battery and fifth-wheel pack. *Ford*

Left: Furniture removal vans and other specialist bodywork – such as the mobile studio for the BBC seen here, on its way to the Los Angeles Olympics – were often built on coach chassis. In this case, it was a Ford R series with 150bhp turbo-charged diesel engine. *Author's Collection*

Left: The British-built Cargo was replaced by the Iveco Cargo – later the EuroCargo. This 75E15 7.5-tonne box van from 1998 is a typical example. The Langley plant had closed in 1997. *Iveco Ford Truck*

GUY

Guy Motors Ltd was founded in 1914 by Sydney Guy, who had been Works Manager at Sunbeam, and a factory was built at Fallings Park, Wolverhampton. Immediately pre-World War 2, Guy produced the 25-cwt to 3-ton Wolf, the 15-cwt Vixen and the 6-ton Otter. The company competed for military vehicle contracts and was rewarded with orders for Ant four-wheeled 15-cwt trucks, which formed the basis of the four-wheel drive Quad-ant. In addition, Guy was able to build some civilian vehicles for official users, including the Vix-ant which combined Vixen and Ant components.

The company re-started production after 1947 with pre-war designs, as anticipated. However, in 1952, the 6-ton Otter was fitted with a new all-steel cab and, in 1953, a short-wheelbase tractor version was offered. In 1954, the 8-ton Big Otter was introduced, together with the first of the long line of Invincible models with four, six and eight-wheeled versions, rated at 12 tons, 20 tons and 24 tons gvw. These were supplemented in 1956 by the first of the forward control Warrior series, either as rigids or tractors, for 6 to 15-tons gvw. From 1958 the Warrior and Invincible shared the same cab design.

Guy Motors spent too much on development during the 1950s (notably of the innovative Wulfrunian bus), which led to the appointment of a receiver at the end of the decade. The company was then taken over by Jaguar Cars Ltd in 1961 and the company name changed to Guy Motors (Europe) Ltd. By 1964, developments of existing models led to the Big J six and eight-wheeled rigids and tractors, designed around a new Cummins V6 engine and intended for motorway operation. However, by then bus production was being run down. In 1966, Jaguar Cars was acquired by the British Motor Corporation and the new group became British Motor Holdings Ltd in December 1966. BMH and Leyland Motors Ltd merged in 1968 to form the British Leyland Motor Corporation Ltd.

The Big J continued to sell well, with around 16,000 chassis produced in all, which kept the factory open for a while. BLMC was partly nationalised in 1975, with the Government creating a new holding company called British Leyland Ltd, which later became BL Ltd in 1978 (and later still BL plc). The management had intended to close Guy Motors in the mid-1970s, but it remained open because of the demand for the Big J.

By the late 1970s, BL was finding it hard to compete with the growing competition from abroad. A rationalisation programme began, during which many of the group's factories were closed. In 1981, the decision was taken to close Guy Motors because the factory lacked the facilities for modern truck production. This was ironic, as Guy Motors was one of the few companies in the BL group that actually made a profit, its order books full for at least 18 months ahead. In spite of this, the factory was closed in August 1982, and 740 jobs were lost.

Production finally ceased in 1979, and the famous Red Indian figure with the slogan 'Feathers in our Cap' no longer adorned the radiators of products from Falllings Park. Such radiator caps are now a treasured memento of the past.

Left: Normal control vehicles were always popular with some operators, like this early post-World War 2 Guy Wolf 2-ton integral van which was part of the Shippam's fleet. *CHC abh829*

Left: This Wolf Diesel, seen during testing, has the same style cab as the Vixen, Otter and other forward control models made during the late 1940s. Most had petrol engines at this time. *CHC abe071*

Above: This Otter Diesel artic tractor in the Whiteways Cider fleet has the later style of the coach-built cab fitted to all the Guy models at the turn of the 1950s. *CHC aaw818*

Left: The all-steel Motor Panels cab replaced Guy's own coach-built style on the smaller models during the mid-1950s, like this Otter Diesel box van. *CHC aay319*

Right: The Guy Invincible eight-wheeler was a move into the heavier weight sector, using some parts from AEC and a version of the Willenhall cab used by BMC, ERF and others at the time. *CHC aac043*

Right: Guy soon introduced its own unmistakable style of cab in 1958 for its heavier models, as seen with this Invincible eight-wheeler. The whole of the upper half was made from GRP and could be removed for maintenance. *CHC abe978*

Right: Tate & Lyle was a big user of Guy lorries for many years, including Warrior box vans like this one at the 1960 Commercial Vehicle Show. Note the later style of front bumpers, compared with the Invincible seen previously. *CHC aab407*

Left: Later Warriors and Invincibles like this 1966 artic tractor unit, one of the last to be made, had a different style of 'long-door' cab. *CHC dai574*

Left: The Jaguar takeover of Guy resulted in the Big J, which appeared as a four, six and eight-wheeled rigid and maximum weight tractor unit. It was a no-frills vehicle, which proved popular with many fleet operators. *PM Photography*

Left: One of the later Big J tractor units – this model proved so popular that the Guy factory stayed open longer than intended by British Leyland – production finally ending in 1982. *PM Photography*

HINO

1967-present

Hino Heavy Industries Ltd was founded in Ohmuri, Tokyo to build heavy diesel trucks, the first of which was a bonneted seven-tonner with four-speed transmission, spiral bevel axle and air brakes. In 1948, the company was reorganised once more and became the Hino Diesel Industry Co Ltd; in 1959 it was reregistered as Hino Motors Ltd. In 1966, the company merged with the Toyota Motor Co, divesting itself of all lighter models to concentrate on heavier types.

It has been suggested that when Robert 'Pino' Harris, who was importing Guy lorries to Ireland, found that Guy were being taken over by Leyland Motors and he no longer had anything to sell. Instead, he began importing and assembling a then unknown Japanese truck: the Hino. Another story goes that Leyland wanted to impose a uniform marketing style at odds with Harris's individualistic approach. After seeing a Hino truck exhibited at a motor show, he thus began an intense courtship of the Japanese to win the assembly and sales franchise for Ireland

In 1967, J. Harris (Assemblers) Ltd began importing, assembling and distributing Hino Trucks under licence from premises in Naas Road, Dublin. These were much the same as the Japanese-built Hinos but, during the 1970s, an 8x4 rigid chassis was developed for the Irish tipper market from the existing forward control 6x4 tipper chassis. By 1981, various Irish-built models were being offered on the British mainland.

Today, distribution of Hino Trucks is via a dealer network in Ireland and the UK. The company assembles 300 light-duty, 500 medium-duty and 700 heavy-duty vehicles. The 300 is available in standard, wide, and crew-cab variants, plus the Hybrid and tipper variants. The 500 is available in the 10,500-26,000kg gvw range and the 700 is available in four wheelbases. There is also a high-roof model.

Above: Hino lorries assembled in Dublin were first imported into the British mainland in 1981. These two tippers were on display at the Tipcon exhibition in 1982. On the left is an eight-wheeler, and on the right a six-wheeler. *CHC aao200*

Left: This is an interesting shot of an Irish Hino 6x4 with a tanker body, delivering Esso fuels in Dublin in the late 1970s. *CHC abm331*

INTERNATIONAL

1965-68

In 1930, International Harvester started the production of agricultural implements at a factory on Wheatley Hall Road in Doncaster. In September 1949, a new factory in the Carr Hill area produced its first tractor, built from parts shipped from the USA. By 1965, assembly of British-built tractors was concentrated at the Carr Hill works, which then began production of International Loadstar trucks as well. By the time of their launch, three models were available: 7 or 8 tons, as well as a 19-ton 15-cwt artic.

According to a Motor Transport advertisement, the Loadstar was 'Tough – Powerful – Solid – Dependable ... low initial investment with unrivalled performance and long-lasting economy.' The right-hand drive vehicles were assembled using some imported US parts, but were modified to satisfy the UK Construction & Use regulations and usually fitted with Perkins engines as well.

One haulier, Bradley Transport Services of Accrington, was said to have a fleet of over 100 running and they were certainly worked hard, with 20-ton payloads behind Perkins-powered tractors with single-axle trailers.

A range of forward control (cab-over-engine) models was planned and at least reached prototype stage, as various chassis with Bedford TK-lookalike cabs were exhibited (for example, at the 1965 Brussels Show). However, the project was evidently not sufficiently profitable and all production ceased in 1968. The factory eventually closed in late 2007.

Above: This International Harvester Model 65 Pay Hauler dumptruck was exhibited at a Crystal Palace construction equipment exhibition, around 1962. It used an IH engine. *CHC aag265*

Left: This International Harvester Loadstar 1700 had a 12ft 7in chassis and was priced in 1966 at £1,593. It was photographed on test with a York W2 trailer loaded to 18 tons gvw. The shortest wheelbase Loadstar at the time had an 11ft 7in wheelbase but, in order to achieve optimum loadings on the three axles of the outfit, as the semitrailer was 32ft long, the 12ft 7in-wheelbase version was selected instead – the longest wheelbase tractor then available in the UK. It had a 114bhp Perkins 6.354 engine, five-speed gearbox and optional Eaton two-speed axle. Note the Leyland Comet behind it. *Ian Allan Library*

ISUZU

1996-present

In 1996, Leyland Trucks Manufacturing, then building the 45 and 55 on behalf of DAF at the Leyland Assembly Plant (LAP), entered into an agreement with Isuzu Motors Europe Ltd. From 1996 until autumn 1999, Leyland would assemble Isuzu N Series light trucks under a manufacturing contract with the Japanese company. They were then sold through Isuzu Truck (UK) Ltd's separate sales network in England, Wales and Scotland.

After the acquisition of Leyland by PACCAR, announced in June 1998, the agreement was cancelled (presumably on notice) and Sandbach Engineering subsequently announced in December that an agreement had been reached to build 2,000 Isuzu N Series trucks in Sandbach at the new factory in Middlewich, Cheshire. It was good news, it was claimed, for around 200 workers at ERF's factories in Middlewich and Sandbach, who were then working just four days a week because of a slump in orders. Managers said that the contract would provide job security to the 800-strong workforce and that ERF had fought-off stiff competition to win the order. Isuzu made a press statement: 'We looked at a number of manufacturers in Britain and mainland Europe before coming to a decision. We were most impressed by the ERF system of production and by the quality of build of the trucks. And we are confident that this arrangement for ERF to build the Isuzu N Series will be of great benefit to both companies.

Managing Director John Bryant said: 'We have the capacity to handle the Isuzu trucks by setting up a specific production line within our present facilities. The extra assembly activity will ensure better productivity and overhead utilisation. ERF's philosophy of building quality, custom trucks allows us to effectively assimilate Isuzu's production requirements.'

In June 1999, ERF confirmed plans to relocate its truck-building operation from Sandbach to a single site at Middlewich, with work on the £25m manufacturing facility due to start that same summer. ERF was then sold by its Canadian parent, Western Star, to MAN of Germany for about £110 million in February 2000. It was then announced a year later that Middlewich had opened and would build 3,000 vehicles in a single shift. However, in September 2001, ERF was quoted as planning to shed 370 jobs as part of a cost-cutting campaign by parent company MAN. Then, in March 2002, ERF would relocate its assembly operation to Germany and parent company MAN sought an alternative use for the Middlewich factory. In June 2003, ERF shed a further 67 jobs at its truck plant in Middlewich, following the decision to relocate production to Germany.

However, with the closure of the Middlewich factory in July 2002, assembly of Isuzu trucks ended. Since then, N Series (and now F Series) trucks have been imported from a CKD assembly plant in Portugal and marketed through Isuzu Truck (UK), based in Hatfield, Hertfordshire.

Right: Leyland Assembly Plant produced Isuzu N Series trucks for Isuzu Europe from 1996-99. ERF then took over from around September 1999, but finished towards the end of 2001. This Isuzu NQR was registered in late 2001 or early 2002, thus representing the last of the Middlewich-assembled N Series trucks. They were assembled alongside the ERF production lines under contract in a small area to one side of the main ECX and ECS assembly lines.
Keith Child/Isuzu Truck (UK) Ltd

JENSEN

1938-57

This well-known marque is more associated with expensive passenger cars or sports cars, although a variety of commercial vehicles was also produced for nearly 20 years. Brothers Richard and Alan Jensen were introduced to George Mason, whose father had an interest in a long-established coachbuilding firm, W. J. Smith & Son Ltd of Carters Green, West Bromwich. The company was not doing well. Mason asked the brothers if they would step in and re-organise the business, the majority of which was the construction of commercial vehicle bodies. They agreed and were appointed joint Managing Directors, with Mason as Chairman. Richard Jensen dealt with the business side of the company and Alan Jensen the practical side of commercial vehicle building.

With the commercial side operating smoothly by 1935, the Jensen brothers set up a small department in one area of the factory to build Ford V8-powered Jensen cars with the company's own bodywork. In March 1936, the company changed its name to Jensen Motors Ltd. Under the new name the car-building department started producing small sports bodies, fitted to Wolseley, Singer, Standard and Morris chassis, plus exclusive modified coachwork for larger cars.

In 1938/9, Jensen diversified into the production of commercial vehicles under the JNSN name, including the manufacture of a series of innovative lightweight trucks intended for conveying long tubing for aircraft, built with aluminium alloys and some Ford components (including engines) for the Reynolds Tube Co of Tyseley. Lorries weighing over 3 tons ulw were restricted to 20mph, but the new design offered a vehicle weighing under 3 tons ulw which could carry a 6-ton load at 30mph.

Immediately post-World War 2, the mass scrapping of aircraft meant that aluminium alloy was readily available and yet there was a shortage of steel. Therefore, in 1946, Jensen came up with an integral commercial vehicle design that combined the main frame and superstructure in light alloys. This allowed the vehicle a 23ft platform length within the maximum permitted overall length of 27ft 6in. The distinctively stylised JNSN front radiator grille was used on a variety of vehicles including pantechnicons, dropside lorries and even a few buses. The engines were Perkins P6 diesels and the entire radiator, clutch and gearbox could be removed in a half-hour and a new unit installed in two hours.

However, the post-war raising of speed limits meant that lightweight vehicles were unnecessary. Steel became more freely available and could be repaired cheaply in the case of accidents, unlike aluminium alloy – though of course this did not rust! The company then ceased commercial production, concentrating instead on passenger cars and car bodies for other manufacturers.

Jensen also designed a mechanical horse, the articulated Jen-Tug, which eventually went into production in 1948 and was first supplied to British Railways. By 1951, the Jen-Tug used an Austin A40 engine and there was also a battery-powered version called the Jen-Helecs. However, they were restricted by a low payload, and only a few were built.

Left: This shot was taken at the first post-war London Commercial Vehicle Exhibition in 1948. It shows a 5-ton pantechnicon behind a Jensen JLP1 single-deck bus chassis.
CHC aau316

Left: This 6-ton dropside in use with a West Country brewery has a late-1947 Cardiff registration.
CHC aas359

Left: This Jen-Tug 'mechanical horse' was tested by *Commercial Motor* magazine and displays a 1946/7 West Bromwich registration. Note the complete lack of traffic!
CHC aau050

Below: Two new Jensen dropside six-tonners, photographed by *Commercial Motor* on an early post-World War 2 visit to the West Bromwich works.
CHC aap523

KARRIER

1908-80

Clayton & Co of Huddersfield was founded in 1904 and started making Karrier cars in 1908. The company name changed to Karrier Motors Ltd in 1920. Karrier introduced the Cob three-wheeled mechanical horse in 1930, but financial difficulties in 1934 caused the company to be taken over by the Rootes Group, through its subsidiary Humber Ltd. The following year, production of commercial vehicles was transferred to Luton alongside the Commer range.

During World War 2, Karrier-badged 4x4 lorries and gun tractors and six-wheeled gun tractors were built, alongside wartime versions of the pre-war Bantams for essential users (who included various local authorites and Rootes' Sunbeam-Talbot plant in west London).

After the war, the 30-cwt and 2-ton Bantam models recommenced production, acquiring a new cab in 1948 and being joined by the 3 to 4-ton CK3, which proved ideal for municipal work. In 1950, they were superseded by new models with underfloor engines and all-steel cabs, very similar to those fitted to Commer forward control vehicles. The new Bantam, which continued with smaller wheels, and the larger Gamecock continued Karrier's association with local authority vehicles, as well as being ideal for local collection and delivery work.

In 1955, the new Boscombe Road, Dunstable plant opened and production of Commer and Karrier vehicles moved to there from Luton. In addition to the Commer Walk-Thru, there were new Karrier-badged versions replacing the BFK Karrier-badged version of the Commer BF range. The Bantam was updated again in 1963.

Control of Karrier, along with Commer, passed to Chrysler UK Ltd in 1973 (as already discussed in the chapter on Commer). As with some previous models, the lower-capacity Commer Commandos were badged as Karriers.

In 1978, PSA (Peugeot-Citroën) reached agreement with the Chrysler Corporation for the purchase and takeover of its principal European operations. Then, in June 1978, after 30 years' continuous production, the last Karrier Bantam left the line to make way for the new Dodge 50, although some municipal vehicles later acquired Karrier nameplates. In 1980, Renault acquired the truck-manufacturing facilities in the UK and, in January 1981, Renault and PSA combined, resurrecting Singer Motors Ltd and changing its name to Karrier, which sold Dodge trucks with Renault badges. By 1983, Karrier Motors Ltd had become Renault Truck Industries Ltd.

Left: Post-World War 2, Karrier Motors' models remained much the same as during the pre-war period, although the demand for municipal vehicles was fulfilled by the Bantam and CK3 – which had a redesigned cab and a 9ft 3in wheelbase, with an 11ft 3in 4-ton chassis and a dropside body available. This Karrier CK3, with a Yorkshire 750-gallon gully emptier body, was commissioned by the Sunderland Corporation and photographed in early 1946. Improvements had increased efficiency by some 33⅓% over the pre-war design. *Karrier*

Right: The Bantam was carried over into the post-war period. This 1946 5-ton 6ft wheelbase tractor could couple automatically to a special van body trailer, with movable partitions and side and rear roller shutters. *Karrier*

Right: This 30-cwt Bantam (No 1040) was new in January 1949, specially designed by T. Wall & Sons Ltd of west London, Manchester and Edinburgh. (The body may have been built in the company's Acton workshops.) It was used for collecting refrigerators for servicing and had a special winch that allowed two men to load and unload heavy units. *Ian Allan Library*

Right: The Karrier-Yorkshire Utility in this June 1954 view has a 750-gallon Gully Emptying Appliance and a Perkins P6 diesel engine. The cab is identical to that of the 1954/5 Commer Superpoise Mk IIIA and synchromesh gearbox. It must have been built at Biscot Road, Luton, as the new Dunstable plant (to which assembly would move) did not start production for some months. By 1952, there was a Karrier-Yorkshire RSC, which was an swb left-hand drive road sweeper collector that used a similar grille but a much narrower bonnet, with a Superpoise six-cylinder petrol engine. *Karrier*

Left: In 1951, the Bantam was updated by a new version that used the Rootes subsidiary British Light Steel Pressings' new cab, as used on the QX but with a different radiator grille, initially either a 45 or 48bhp low-compression version of the Humber Hawk car engine. The rigids were rated at 2-3 tons. There was also a redesigned and strengthened riveted-construction frame. This January 1957 shot is of a 2-ton Bantam with a special 400 cu ft Luton van body, in the fleet of printers and stationers W. Straker Ltd. The body was by BSA Group subsidiary Hooper (Coachbuilders) & Co Ltd of Park Royal, northwest London, more famous for its luxury car bodies. The engine options by then were the 53.5bhp petrol or 54bhp light diesel engines. *Karrier*

Left: The Gamecock 3-4 tonner was announced at the 1952 Commercial Motor Show, replacing the CK-3. Its engine would either be the 85bhp Humber light six petrol or, by 1954, the 105bhp TS3 diesel from the QX. The same BLSP cab was used but mounted higher than the Bantam, with eight rather than six wheel studs on the larger wheels, although the Gamecock could also be ordered with smaller wheels for low-loading bodywork. At the same time a new compression refuse collector was offered, the Karrier-Transport Loadmaster, with a 20-25 cu yd capacity body provided by Glover, Webb and Liversidge Ltd of London – in this case on a 1954-registered West Ham Corporation vehicle with a crew-cab. *Karrier*

Right: The Karrier Kob 'mechanical horse' was dropped after World War 2, but the new Bantam was offered as a 4 to 5-ton tractor-trailer unit. Petrol engines were only offered initially but, in September 1956, the Bantam became available with the 54bhp 2.26-litre light diesel that was also used in the Commer BF/Karrier BFK light commercial models. However, this 1957 tractor-trailer had the 53.5bhp petrol engine, four-speed synchromesh gearbox and robust rear axle with full-floating shafts. It also had the J-type coupling gear (although the BK type was optional) that allowed automatic coupling and detaching of semitrailers without the driver having to leave the cab. *Karrier*

Above: The Bantam was updated with the single-piece screen on the BSLP cab and remained in limited production until the early 1970s. It was popular with local authorities and companies that carried out door-to-door deliveries, like Corona. *Ian Allan Library*

Left: The 8-ton Commer CA series with Sankey cab was introduced in 1962 in two wheelbases, replacing the QX. The Karrier Gamecock continued to be available, corresponding with the Commer VA models. In 1964, the CA was replaced by the CB, before the CC replaced them both in 1965. The vehicle in the photograph is thought to be a 1964 Gamecock with seven-seat crew CB-style Sankey cab and Blenheim continuous loading refuse collector, No 1 with the Borough of Barking (which became the London Borough of Barking in 1965). It is coupled to a trailer. *Rootes Motors*

Right: This is one of the nine 1956-built Bantams that were acquired by the BBC in 1956, bodied by Mickelover Transport. It was photographed in the mid-1960s, when in use as a colour-television demonstration unit. *CHC abl179*

LEYLAND / LEYLAND DAF / DAF

1907-present

The vast British Leyland Truck & Bus division, which has swallowed up so many manufacturers, can trace its history back to a company which made steam wagons in 1896. Their first petrol-engined vehicle appeared in 1904 for a 30-cwt payload, then followed the 3-ton Y Type and 3-ton X Type in 1907. The firm established itself in 1912 with the normal control 3-ton Subsidy-type vehicle, of which 5,932 were built up to November 1918 for the Royal Flying Corps. This vehicle became known as the 'RAF type' and refurbished examples were sold to many civilian operators after World War 1.

Leyland has been responsible for many commercial developments over the years. Backed by a team of brilliant engineers such as Sir Henry Spurrier, it thus gained a reputation for great design and reliability. In the 1930s, Leyland was producing freight vehicles with a range extending from the 3-ton normal control model to the eight-wheeled forward control Octopus for 15-ton payloads. Other animals in the Leyland zoo were named Bison, Buffalo, Bull, Beaver, Hippo, Lynx and Steer.

During World War 2, Leyland contributed to the national effort by producing five different types of tank, including the Cromwell and Comet, as well as supplying 1,000 Hippo six-wheelers and other vehicles and munitions for the fighting services.

The first vehicles produced after the war were known as 'Interim Beavers', using parts held in stock at the time. One of the first of the new post-war range was the Comet 75 in 1947, a semi–forward control 6-ton model distinguished by the frontal styling of its Briggs-made cab. Four years later, the Comet 90 model for 7-ton loads was manufactured, remaining in production until 1956. Super Comet forward control models appeared in 1954, with a cab design similar to that of the Leyland Octopus.

Meanwhile, the Octopus had been revived in 1948 as the 22.0/1 model, with many going to the fledgling British Road Services. It shared a forward control cab with the new four-wheeled Beaver and six-wheeled Hippo, updated as the 22.0/4 with the all-steel 'Mouth Organ' cab in 1954, later replaced by the LAD Vista-View in 1958 on the Power-Plus range.

Below: Leyland Motors restarted commercial production soon after the war with the so-called 'Interim Beaver', model 12IB.400, produced using surplus wartime Hippo parts. This 1946 shot is of five of these, which replaced 16-year-old Leylands operated by brewers James Hole & Co Ltd of Newark, Nottinghamshire. By 1948, bonneted Beavers and heavy Hippo tractors were both being built. *Leyland Motors*

Left: From 1948, Leyland was using its new flat front-style cab as demonstrated by this Octopus 22.0/1 8x4. This lorry was new in summer 1950 and appears to be in the London Docks. It was fleet no 101 with millers W. Vernon & Sons of London. The 8-ton payload of Spillers flour could be discharged in 45 minutes by compressed air. *Ian Allan Library*

Right: The Leyland Comet became available early in 1948 and provided a medium-weight alternative to the heavier Beaver. It had a gross weight of 8¾ tons, a 17ft 6in wheelbase and it used a cab from Briggs Motor Bodies Ltd similar to that of the Dodge 100 Series, or used by Fordson Thames and Guy Motors. This 1953-registered tipper was operated by Gubbins and Ball Ltd of Newport, Isle of Wight, and is seen in their hometown. *Ian Allan Library*

In 1951, Leyland acquired Albion Motors, followed by Scammell in 1955 and AEC (which had already acquired Maudslay, Crossley and Thornycroft) in 1962. Leyland also acquired a major shareholding in Bristol Commercial Vehicles in 1965, before Rover/Alvis joined the empire in 1966 and Aveling-Barford a year later. Then, in 1968, Leyland merged with British Motor Holdings, which already had Austin, Morris, Guy and Daimler under its wing, these famous manufacturers all disappearing under the Leyland name.

A completely new design of cab was introduced in 1964. Known as the Ergomatic, it became the standard for the heavier models in the range, including those produced under the Albion and AEC badges.

In 1970, the goods vehicle range was again extended with the introduction of the Bear six-wheeler; two years later, the new Buffalo range of models went up to 32 tons gross. The Marathon range of tractive units and 4x2 rigids for loads up to 32 tons gcw or 44 tons gtw was introduced in 1973; three years later, there was a new Octopus Rigid 8-wheeler.

The lighter weight former BMC vehicles – known since 1968 as the Redline range – were redesigned in 1972, with the Mastiff six-wheeler joining the existing

Mastiff (16 tons, 24 tons and 28 tons), the Boxer (10-16 tons) and the Terrier (6½-9½ tons). These vehicles were all fitted with the G cab design, and the range also incorporated the FG range of lighter vehicles from BMC of 3½-6½ tons. All these models were produced at the Bathgate works in West Lothian.

By the close of 1980, Leyland's range included the T45 Roadtrain with five different models of forward control tractor units, incorporating the new C40 cab design which could also be supplied as a sleeper cab, and the new Leyland Flexitorque engine with a Rolls-Royce or Cummins as an alternative. At the same time, there was a normal control Landtrain built, of which eight models were available from 19-65 tons gvw. Those models were mainly for the export market and superseded the Super Hippo and Super Beaver.

In 1981, a lighter version of the Roadtrain called the Cruiser entered production with a range of three tractor units, fitted with the new slimmer C40 cab and designed for operation up to

34 tons gcw. The Blueline range (the Buffalo, Bison and Lynx) ceased production by 1982.

Later that year a lightweight range also fitted with the C40 cab, called the Freighter, was introduced to replace the Clydesdale (the last of the old Leyland-Albion range) and the Boxer. From 1982, Leyland started to discontinue the Redline range, beginning with the Terrier, followed by the Mastiff and Boxer by 1984. The T45 Freighter range for 16 tonnes gvw

Right: Albion Motors was acquired by Leyland Motors in 1951, Around 1956/7, the Albion factory produced a limited number of six-wheeled prime movers resembling the export Super Hippo, but with a much longer bonnet. They were powered by the Leyland-designed 900 engine built at Albion and were sent down to Leyland as chassis cabs supposedly for Roadtrain use by South African Railways. This six-wheeled van was destined for Rhodesia Railways and was on the Leyland stand at the 1956 London Commercial Motor Show, described in the catalogue as a Hippo.
Ian Allan Library

Right: The original flat-fronted cab was replaced in 1954 by a new 'mouth organ' grille style and used across the forward control range. J. & H. Transport Services (Peckham) Ltd operated a number of diesel-engined Octopus lorries for transporting a variety of loads. In this November 1956 view, SXD 492 is being loaded with large chemical drums.
Ian Allan Library

was available with five different wheelbases and a choice of four engines. One year later, models for 12.3 tonnes gvw and 13.29 tonnes gvw were introduced, followed in August 1983 by models in the 10.81 and 14.75 tonnes gvw ranges. All models were once again available with differing wheelbases and a choice of engines.

The lighter models were replaced by the Roadrunner range, from 6-10 tonnes, in 1984. The range offered four different wheelbase lengths from 10ft 8in to 14ft. All models had a BMC-designed 6.98-litre engine, but this was later changed to a Cummins B series when the Bathgate plant closed in June 1986. All models had a Motor Panels cab derived from the C40.

The ex-Scammell Constructor S26 6x4 24-tonne and 8x4 30-tonne chassis, now fitted with Cummins 11-litre engines, continued to be available. The model was first introduced in 1980 but was supplied with many different engines, the last being the Perkins (ex-Rolls-Royce) Eagle turbo-charged diesel rated at 285bph.

At the Motor Show in 1986, Leyland exhibited a fire appliance – its first for 25 years. Based on the 16-tonne Freighter chassis with a Leyland 400 series engine and automatic transmission, only a few were ever built. The 4x2 Cruiser lightweight tractor unit for 32.5 tonnes gcw was also on show.

Word of talks to merge Leyland with General Motors circulated towards the close of 1985, for the state-owned company was making redundancies among its workforce and did not have the finances to design and produce a replacement for its Roadtrain range, which it had been building since 1980. However, it still came as a shock when, in February 1987, it was announced that DAF had taken control of Leyland.

Left: In this August 1957 view, six-wheeled Hippo 20H/11 was No 1 on the fleet of W. Beardmore & Co Ltd of Glasgow, recently delivered by bodybuilders J. Wilkinson of Edinburgh. The load was a ship's driveshaft weighing over 12 tons, destined for the Clyde shipyards. *Ian Allan Library*

Below: The forward control cab replaced the Briggs normal control type on the Comet in 1956. This Comet ECOS 2/6R was one of a new fleet of motive units and 10-ton semi-trailers with Scammell automatic couplings in 1957, which BRS operated on its Irish ferry service from Preston Docks to Larne in conjunction with associated company Atlantic Steam Navigation Ltd. The latter's Empire Nordic ferry is in the background. *BTC*

The DAF influence made itself felt very soon afterwards, with the closure of the old Scammell plant at Watford. Some of the factories at Leyland were also closed. In addition, DAF components started to be used and vehicles appeared with a 'Leyland DAF' badge.

The new regime soon began to integrate its two ranges, quickly ceasing production of Leyland's own engines in favour of DAF units, themselves derived from Leyland designs. Two of DAF's existing product lines, the 1700 and 1900, were assembled at the Leyland plant in Lancashire, while the newer Leyland range was scaled down and relaunched with DAF model numbers. However, these numbers also indicated that most models on which they appeared would have a shorter production life: DAF was giving its longer-term models numbers ending in '5', while most of the revamped Leylands ended in '0'.

In 1990, the Cummins-engined Freighter reappeared as the Leyland DAF 50; the 6.2-litre DAF-engined Freighter (replacing the Leyland 400-powered version) became the Leyland DAF 70; both the Roadtrain and the eight-wheel Constructor (each powered by DAF's 11.6-litre engine) were badged 'Leyland DAF 80'.

In 1991, the process was continued down the weight range, this time with model numbers clearly intended to suggest a longer working life. The Roadrunner, having secured 25,000 sales, was replaced by the Leyland DAF 45. While the 50, 60, 70 and 80 showed little external difference other than a DAF-style grille in place of the Leyland design, the 45 was more radically distinct. In particular, adoption of the DAF grille eliminated the nearside lower dash window (termed a 'dog' window, as it was about

Above: The Motor Panels Vista-Vue or 'LAD' cab (as it was shared by Leyland, Albion and Dodge) was introduced in 1958. This 1961 Octopus model 240/9 with the long-door version of the LAD had a 140bhp Leyland O.600 diesel engine and was used by Thos Gibb & Co Ltd to transport Aberdeenshire beef and newspaper rolls. The container was removed to transport the rolls. *Ian Allan Library*

Left: By 1961, the Comet became available with the LAD cab, the latter supplemented by the heavier Super Comet 14-ton 14SC and 16-ton 16SC. This Super Comet tractor was new in the autumn of 1961 as No 957 in the Ross Group fleet, the first of several intended for frozen-food distribution. It had a Dyson articulated trailer with a 1,000 cu ft container by Holmes of Preston. *Ross Group*

the right height for a guard dog sitting on the cab floor) on the Roadrunner. A ZF gearbox replaced the Turner gearbox on the previous model.

From 1995, the 45 was joined by the 11 to 15-tonne Leyland DAF 55. This also had a Cummins B Series engine and was launched originally in mainland Europe as a DAF, not sold in the UK for another year. A four-wheel drive truck, using the same cab design, was produced for the British Ministry of Defence as part of the order that effectively sealed the demise of AWD.

DAF also planned to replace the 50, 60, 70 and 80 with a new rigid with a higher cab, to accommodate

its 11.61-litre WS engine. At this time, the plan was to produce the 65 and 85 at the Leyland plant in Lancashire, but DAF ran into severe financial difficulties and was plunged into receivership. For a time, it looked like the remnants of Britain's best-known truck producer would disappear, but instead the company was broken up and sold to separate owners.

Dutch interests bought the main DAF company, and so production of the 65 and 85 went ahead in the Netherlands and Belgium. The Leyland DAF company in the UK was also bought by the new Dutch company. The manufacturing operation at Leyland was sold to its

management, renamed Leyland Trucks Manufacturing and continued producing the 45 (joined from its launch by the 55) on behalf of the new DAF company.

This company also began developing a limited range of Leyland-badged vehicles for some export markets beyond Europe, where it was not covered by the supply contract for DAF. From 1996-99, Leyland Trucks assembled Isuzu light trucks on a manufacturing contract with the Japanese company, for sale through Isuzu's separate UK sales network.

There was also a management buy-in that took control of the axle and chassis component plants at Glasgow and Leyland, forming a new company with a name steeped in its heritage (Albion Automotive), while the research and development facilities in Lancashire went to another management team. Albion Automotive has since come under American ownership, as have both Leyland and DAF.

In 1996, PACCAR acquired DAF and the Leyland DAF sales business, with the Seattle-based group going on to buy Leyland Trucks in 1998. This gave PACCAR a much larger foothold in the European truck market than it had achieved since buying Foden in 1980. The purchase of DAF also provided it with its own engine manufacturing capacity, even though it has continued to use engines from the major US-owned manufacturers in its American and Foden ranges. (PACCAR had been keen to buy Leyland when the British Government was selling its controlling stake in the business in 1986/7.)

One immediate effect of the takeovers was to terminate Leyland's contract with Isuzu, which went to ERF for a time, and for Leyland to cease producing vehicles for export markets not served by DAF. Production of right-hand-drive 65, 75 and 85 models was gradually transferred to the UK, with Foden building the 65 from 1997 until all production moved to Leyland in 2000, including Foden's. This left DAF's Benelux plants with more space to meet growing demand from other left-hand drive markets.

The last vestiges of the Leyland range were destined to disappear from 2001 onwards, with the introduction of new Leyland-built LF45 and LF55 7.5-18 tonne models. Powered by 135-250hp four- and six-cylinder Cummins ISBe engines, they were developed in a European Engine Alliance between Cummins, Iveco and Fiat-owned tractor manufacturer Case New Holland. In place of the previous model's Motor Panels cabs, the LF45 and LF55 use a French-built Renault cab as previously fitted on the latter's Midlum models. (Renault's own truck business is now owned by Volvo.)

PACCAR has dropped the Leyland name from all trucks which had been sold as Leyland DAF in the UK or as DAFs everywhere else. Thus one of the most famous names in British truck manufacturing has disappeared.

Today, DAF Ltd has its headquarters in Thame, Oxon. From 7.5 to 44 tonnes, DAF is the market leader across all weight sectors in the UK. The right-hand drive LF (LF45 and LF55) and CF (CF75 and CF85) series, plus the XF105 rigid and tractor chassis, are all built by PACCAR-owned Leyland Trucks. It is the largest producer and exporter of trucks in the UK, with the capacity for manufacturing 25,000 DAF trucks each year. The 600,000 sqm plant is considered to be one of the most modern, flexible and efficient in Europe. Today, DAF lorries account for a major proportion of the UK heavy commercial market.

Above: This 1964-registered Beaver tipper was specially constructed with a 10ft wheelbase for George Webb Ltd of Cambridge. The engine was the 140bhp Leyland O.600 driving through a seven-speed gearbox with overdrive and crawler gear. The all-steel low-height body had a Edbro U.47 heavy-duty twin underfloor tipping gear. It was photographed being loaded by a Priestman shovel. *Ian Allan Library*

Left: The tilting Ergomatic cab made by Sankey was launched by Leyland in 1964 as a replacement for the LAD cab. Also used by AEC and Albion, it saw its last use in 1981. This early 1967-registered Octopus tipper was used by Stirlingshire County Council for roadworks. *Leyland Motors*

Left: This 1967-registered Beaver tractor was used by Huntley & Palmers (by then part of Associated Biscuit Manufacturers Ltd, which became Associated Biscuits in 1969) of Reading for biscuit and cake shipments. *Leyland Motors*

Below: The 16-ton gvw Super Comet 16SCT was introduced in 1965, a short time after the Ergomatic-cabbed heavy-duty models. For export there was also a 14-ton gvw model. Super Comet 14CJS with the fixed 'Ergomatic' cab was available from around 1966. This was also used by the 13-ton gvw Comet 13CJS that finally replaced the LAD-cabbed 13C models. Seen in line in late 1968 are six Super Comets new to the Ministry of Public Building and Works, with bodywork by Firth-Vickers Stainless Steel Ltd of Sheffield. *Firth-Vickers*

Left: This is the first of a series of experimental gas-turbine lorries built over the years by Leyland Motors. This vehicle was displayed at the 1968 London Commercial Motor Show (the same year Leyland merged with BMC to form the British Leyland Motor Corporation) and featured a redesigned version of the 'Ergomatic' cab. One surviving prototype, similar to this one, has been restored to running order. *Ian Allan Library*

Middle: In mid-1964, the cab of the Austin/Morris WE was revised to become the WF, gaining twin headlamps and a one-piece windscreen. Customer demand ensured that the WF range remained in production until it was effectively replaced for export markets by the smallest Landmaster in 1981. In 1970, when production of the remaining BMC-based trucks (FG, WF, Laird and Boxer) was consolidated at the Leyland Motors (Scotland) Ltd Bathgate plant, these models were rebadged as Leyland to bring them into line as the parent company's Redline range, while the Leyland-designed products were known as Blueline. This official 1970 shot is of a Redline WF 4x2. The range consisted of 3.6-11.6 tons gvw, with a choice of engines. *BLMC*

Left: After the 1968 merger, the BMC Pilot cab was given a mild makeover to form the basis of Leyland's Bathgate-built Laird and Terrier light trucks, and on the heavier models in the 1970-originated Redline range, such as the Boxer and Clydesdale, and the 16-ton Mastiff, built by Leyland (Glasgow) at the Albion plant. This launch shot shows a Terrier 4x2 rigid with dropside body. The range consisted of 6.5, 7.5, 8.5 and 9.9-tonners, with a choice of engines and 16in or 20in wheels. The Pilot cab was replaced by the 1975-80 G series. *BLMC*

Above: Leyland adopted an improved second version of the Ergomatic cab which differed from the AEC version, sitting higher to clear the new engine types. This official shot shows a spring 1972-registered Buffalo 4x2 tractor running at 32 tons gvw with the Leyland D10 turbocharged engine. It was new to R.W. Almond & Co. Ltd of Formby, Liverpool. Note the redesigned grille. *BLMC*

Left: This photograph dates from the summer of 1972 and shows a new Super Mastiff 2600 6x4 26-ton gvw tipper, which had a Perkins B8-510 engine. Note the later variant on the Pilot cab. *BLMC*

Above: The revised Ergomatic cab is also seen on this Leyland 500-engined Lynx 4x2 Haulage chassis running at 16 tons gvw. It was new in 1972 to Pierpoint & Bryant Ltd of Latchford, near Warrington, Cheshire. *BLMC*

Left: The Bathgate-built cab was known as the G Series from around 1973, with a four-slot air intake on the Terrier and eight slots on the larger models. Above this was a chrome-plated grille panel (although this was sometimes painted matt-black, in body colour or to match a company's livery), and above that the large Leyland lettering. This Redline Boxer 1000 has a second steering axle added by Primrose to enhance tolerance on axle loading during multi-drop work. On nationalisation in 1975, Leyland Commercials became part of the autonomous Truck & Bus Division. *Leyland*

Right: This July 1977 shot is of a late-model Octopus with the later variant of the Ergomatic cab. It was in service with animal feedstuffs manufacturers Nitrovit Ltd of Parbold, Lancashire, and had a bulk-blower body by Seadyke with a Wade blower and Edbro tipping gear. *Leyland*

Right: The Marathon was introduced to compete with the heavyweight Volvos and Scanias. The engine options included the AEC six-cylinder AV760 (which was turbocharged and designated the TL12), a 200bhp Leyland L11 and Cummins 250/330bhp 10 and 14-litre engines. The cab was a reworked version of the 'Ergomatic' tilt cab, heavily modified with different lower panels and raised height, available in day and sleeper cab form. Production began in 1973, when various shortcomings were noted. In 1977, the Marathon 2 was launched to address some of the criticisms of the earlier vehicle. Relatively few Marathons of any types were sold before production ended in 1979, with the introduction of the T45 Roadtrain range of vehicles. This 1975/6-registered Marathon coupled to a Massey trailer was in service with Ross Foods Ltd of Grimsby and used to convey over 16 tons of frozen foods to ports throughout Europe. *Leyland*

Right: Leyland Vehicles Ltd was created in 1978. In 1979, the Buffalo 2 used the final version of the Ergomatic cab with a sleeper extension. This tractor was used to transport Panasonic electrical goods and had the TL11 turbocharged engine, whereas the Buffalo had the 500. The naturally aspirated L11 and turbo TL11 were basically an updated O.680 power unit. The Bison 2 6x4 with 'Ergomatic' cab had the TL11A engine. *Ian Allan Library*

Left: In October 1980 the G Series cab was facelifted as the Super-G cab, bringing it into line with the T45. Note the matt-black grille and Leyland panel above it. This Super Mastiff six-wheeler is demonstrating its off-road capabilities. *Ian Allan Library*

Below: The T45 range was announced at the end of the 1970s, the C40 cab designed jointly between Leyland, BRS and Ogle Design. In September 1979, the new £33 million Leyland Assembly Plant (or LAP) was opened on the outskirts of Leyland, Lancashire, to produce the new model, which is now the home of DAF Trucks. This Constructor model 30-21 eight-wheeled tipper – with a chassis based on the Scammell Routeman and an Anthony Carrimore body – was in service with the Amey Roadstone Company. *Anthony Carrimore*

Right: The 1980-90 Roadtrain replaced the Marathon 2, with engine options initially including the AEC-based TL12 Flexitorque, the Rolls-Royce (then Perkins) Eagle 265/300 and the Cummins 290 L10 and 350 14-litre, coupled to a Spicer SST10 or Eaton transmission. The TL12 was dropped early in the production run and fleet buyers seem to have selected the Rolls engines. The Roadtrain was available in day and sleeper-cabbed form, and in high and low-datum versions; high-datum versions were intended as long-haul vehicles with higher-mounted cabs and more internal space. Built in 1981, this tractor with day-cab was in service with William Low Supermarkets. *Ian Allan Library*

Below: This is an official shot of a six-wheeled T45 Constructor 24-15 model with tipper body, which replaced the various earlier six-wheeled tipper and mixer chassis. *Ian Allan Library*

Left: In February 1980, Leyland Vehicles announced the Cruiser range of three tractor units fitted with the 'slim' version of the C45 cab and designed for operations up to 34 tonnes gvw. *Leyland*

Left: The 7.5 tonnes gross non-HGV Roadrunner was the smallest vehicle in the T45 range and one of the most popular commercial vehicles on the market during the late 1980s. The kerb-side window is just visible on this curtain-sided distribution vehicle. *CHC aap497*

Left: In 1987, DAF Trucks took a 60% controlling share in Leyland Trucks and Freight-Rover, which became DAF NV. The T45 7.5-ton Roadrunner and heavier Freighter, which had been introduced in 1980, were rebadged 'Leyland DAF' in 1987 with other Leyland lorries. This 160bhp turbo-diesel Freighter 14.16 was one of seven, together with a Roadrunner 8.13 that Boots Co PLC acquired in 1989/90 to add to its fleet. *Ian Allan Library*

Above: The Leyland Landtrain was closely related to the Scammell S24 and offered in various weight categories, notably for export markets. *Leyland Vehicles*

Right: This 1991 Leyland DAF FA45.130 was fitted with a Scarab Major hydrostatic drive 5000 roadsweeper body. *Leyland Trucks*

Above: This 1990/91 Leyland DAF 80 Series 330ATi – in service with a bulk tipping trailer for grain merchant Sidney Banks of Sandy in Bedfordshire, always a Leyland operator – represents the transitional period after the DAF takeover, when later Leyland Roadtrains were badged as 'Leyland DAF'.
PM Photography

Left: A modern product of the Leyland Assembly Plant (LAP), this DAF LF, replacement for the Leyland DAF 55 as a maximum weight four-wheeler, is in service with Greggs the bakers.
PM Photography

MANTON AND RUTLAND

1945-57

Manton Motors Ltd was established by Arthur C. Manton, who came from his namesake village of Manton in England's smallest county, Rutland. By 1938, the company had a Commer main dealership and Perkins diesel-engine distribution centre in Addiscombe, Croydon. Advertisements offered six-wheeled conversions from Unipower (Universal Power Drives Ltd of Perivale, Middlesex) and Scammell, which were tested by the War Department for Field Artillery Tractors, although 4x4 became the preferred option. A January 1939 advert detailed an 11-ton payload Commer (ulw 3 tons 19-cwt 3qrt) with Scammell bogie conversion and auxiliary gearbox (providing eight speeds), which retailed at £879 for the chassis, plus £50 tax.

Manton also advertised diesel conversions, using Perkins P6 engines on Albion, Bedford, Commer, Dodge, Leyland, Morris and other makes, as well as 'repairs and maintenance to all makes of oil engines'.

Arthur's son Frank joined his father's business, with its Commer agency, after war service in the Navy. In 1946, however, he set up his own car and commercial vehicle repair business in Croydon. As a consequence of the governmental 'export or die' policy, he subsequently decided he would design and build new lorries.

The 8-ton gvw vehicles were initially badged as 'Manton', powered by Perkins P6 diesel engines. Sales went well in Spain and limits on sales by one agent resulted in further vehicles being sold as 'MTN' (ManToN). Exports went around the world, including to the Indian subcontinent and the Far East.

To avoid clashing with Commer sales, the lorry-manufacturing business was transferred to new premises in 1951 under a new name, Motor Traction Ltd, with vehicles badged 'Rutland' and, in 1955, to nearby New Addington, until it went out of business in 1957. Manton Motors Ltd remained and was subsequently sold to Dees of Croydon, continuing until 2001. The service station is now owned by Tesco and the

Below: This photograph was one of several taken by *Commercial Motor* of Motor Traction vehicles being road tested. The vehicle is captioned as a Rutland 10-tonner and shows a left-hand drive chassis with the distinctive radiator the company used. The picture was taken in Blackhorse Lane, Croydon, as the Perkins-engined vehicle is exiting Teevan Road, just over the bridge from Morland Road where Manton Motors Ltd was initially located. *CHC 00799*

workshops by tyre company Nationwide Autocentres Ltd. Rutland Works in New Addington is still standing and used by an engineering firm.

Motor Traction offered an amazingly wide range of commercial vehicles, covering almost every conceivable type from a one-ton Perkins-engined van through 2 to 3-ton payloads up to a projected TH10716 Rigid eight-wheeler at 24-tons gvw. Two, three and four axles were, in theory at least, available, with both normal control and forward control chassis. Indeed, one source suggests that the company offered over 50 different types, including 4x4s and special mobile-crane chassis, plus the Clipper coach chassis.

Interesting choices of names included the Toucan five-six-tonner, Albatross six/seven-tonner, four and six-wheeled Stuka and four-wheel and twin-steer Eagle six/seven-tonner, some with Gardner 4LW engines, plus Condor four-wheeled and twin-steer, and 8-ton Troubadour lorries. Motor Traction would fit almost any engine and driveline the customer required, including Perkins, Gardner, Meadows and AEC engines, and David Brown gearboxes.

Cabs were custom-built by almost any coachbuilder, although most used Boalloy or Bonallack cabs, including a 'crew-cab', although there were also Motor Panels cabs as used by Guy and Thornycroft. Tipping-gear bodies by Bonallack and Pilot emphasised the use of proprietary components. Girling hydraulic and Neate vacuum brakes are also known to have been fitted.

Production figures were destined to remain low, some even being one-offs, doubtlessly the main reason why the company went out of business in 1957.

Above: This photograph was uncaptioned but was evidently taken at one of Frank Manton's business premises. The sign on the wall says, 'MANTON MOTORS ENGINE OVERHAUL DEPARTMENT', which suggests it was in Teevan Road, Croydon. This 6 to 7-ton chassis has a brand-new cab. Note the twin fuel tanks and the split prop-shaft to the rear axle. *CHC 00975*

Right: This Rutland Troubadour 8-ton chassis was tested by *Commercial Motor* and is seen passing a White Hart hotel. Note the lhd, suggesting it was an export model. The Troubadour was advertised in CM in June 1955 as available with either the 9.6 or the 7.7-litre AEC engine and AEC transmission. *CHC aaw172*

Above: This is a Manton Condor on test by *Commercial Motor*, having apparently been loaded by North Cheshire Motors Ltd of Warrington. In December 1952 it was stated that the Condor 7/8-tonner was the only current production chassis at the time with a Meadows 5.43-litre engine as standard, with a Meadows five-speed gearbox. *CHC abd475*

Above: Another Rutland four-wheeler 6/7-tonner on test by *Commercial Motor*, this time at a favourite spot at Succombs Hill, Warlingham, Surrey. The very smart cab was also used on front-steer six-wheel chassis. *CHC abd626*

Above: This Manton five-tonner was also tested in the south of England by *Commercial Motor*, seen here at the very quiet junction of the A22 from London to Eastbourne via Croydon, where the B2028 and B2026 also intersect. Note the RAC box on the right. *CHC abf736*

Above: This Rutland had a Perkins diesel engine and was operated by haulage contractor E. Pedder of Dunstable. It also had a Bonallack Dekaloy lightweight body and a ulw of under 3 tons, seen here photographed at Watford in July 1955. *Ian Allan Library*

Left: These two Rutland chassis were parked in London Docks awaiting shipment to Jamaica. *Ian Allan Library*

MAUDSLAY

1903-54

The Maudslay Motor Co Ltd was founded in Parkside, Coventry in 1903 and taken over by a new, similarly named public company in 1907. After World War 1, the company concentrated on commercial and passenger-carrying vehicles.

The company shared the suffering of many other commercial concerns in the Great Depression that followed the 1929 Wall Street Crash. Production dropped to a mere 50 vehicles a year. Civilian production ended with the outbreak of war in 1939 and was replaced by war work, mostly at Great Alne, near Alcester – though some continued at what became Castle Maudslay, which was bombed.

Post-World War 2, the lorry and PSV designs which had been proposed immediately pre-war were belatedly introduced. They consisted of the 6-ton four-wheeled Mogul, 7 cu yd Militant tipper, 10-ton rigid twin-steer six wheeled Mustang, 13-ton rigid six-wheeled Maharajah, 13-ton Maharanee tractor unit and the Meritor, a 15-ton rigid eight-wheeled chassis originally named the Mikado (as well as luxury coaches, such as the Marathon). Castle Maudslay at Alcester would make the components, and

these would be taken to the Parkside, Coventry works for vehicle assembly.

However, in 1948, Maudslay was acquired by the Associated Equipment Co Ltd (see AEC chapter), becoming part of the new holding company, Associated Commercial Vehicles (ACV) Ltd. For a few years afterwards, Maudslay produced chassis to its own and AEC's specification, badged either as AEC or, in certain cases, Maudslay. In the early 1950s, the Parkside factory was sold to Cornercroft Engineering and all production transferred to Castle Maudslay. Production finally ceased in 1954, although ACV still had a Maudslay exhibit at the Commercial Motor Show in 1956 and 1958, in order to double its space.

The Castle Maudslay plant continued to supply components to AEC, then the Leyland and finally British Leyland group in the USA for axle and brake production, until it was acquired (along with Maudslay Motor Co) in 1972 by Rockwell Standard. In 1986, Rockwell sold the John Thompson Motor Pressings works but retained the axle bay run from Maudslay's Alcester factory. The plant eventually closed on 22 May 1987.

Right: Brewers Flower & Sons Ltd (founded 1831) of Stratford-upon-Avon acquired this Maudslay Mogul Mk II as a brewer's dray. This March 1946 photograph shows it as fleet No 15. *Ian Allan Library*

Above: This view is dated April 1949 and shows a recent delivery of three Mogul Mk IIs supplied by the Ryland Garage of Birmingham. Alfred T. Hartshorne Ltd of Wednesbury had been using 'Maudslays' since 1928, and these vehicles were given fleet Nos. 49, 50 and 51. *Ian Allan Library*

Left: This 'Chinese Six' twin-steer Mustang had been recently delivered in August 1950 to RAH Transporters Ltd of Newcastle upon Tyne. It was supplied by the northern distributor Oswald Tillotson. *Ian Allan Library*

Above: This 1949-registered eight-wheeled Meritor was photographed in London's Royal Albert Docks in March 1951 with a load of corrugated sheeting. It was No 60 in the fleet of newly nationalised haulier Fred Robinson (BTC) Ltd of Stockton-on-Tees. *Ian Allan Library*

Above: A number of Maudslays were produced during the early 1950s which were basically corresponding AEC models fitted with a Maudslay badge. At least in some cases, this was done in order to gain extra stand space at the commercial-vehicle shows. *CHC aar081*

Above: This 1950-registered Meritor tanker was No 8 on the fleet of Wholesale Kerosene Distributors Ltd. *Ian Allan Library*

MORRIS-COMMERCIAL / MORRIS

1924-68

Morris-Commercial Cars Ltd was founded in 1924, when William Morris (later Lord Nuffield) personally bought the assets of E.G. Wrigley & Co after it went into receivership. Until then, a small number of commercial variants of Morris cars were built at the Morris plant at Cowley. Morris-Commercial production took place at the newly acquired plant in Soho, Birmingham until 1932, when it moved to Adderley Park, Birmingham. In 1936, the separate company was sold to Morris Motors Ltd, becoming part of the Nuffield Group. The 'Morris-Commercial' name was used on the vehicles until 1956, when it was replaced by 'Morris'.

During World War 2, Adderley Park produced military lorries, gun tractors and specialised vehicles, as well as some pre-war designs. From 1948, developments in the range catered for higher payloads. Several alternative engines were offered, including the 100hp six-cylinder petrol and a new diesel manufactured in association with Saurer. The 10-cwt Morris-Commercial J-type forward control van was introduced in 1949 (rebadged Morris, along with an Austin version in 1957) and two years later the restyled 2/3-ton and 5-ton models were called Equiload.

In 1952, the Nuffield Group merged with Austin Motor Co Ltd to form the British Motor Corporation (BMC) and standardisation began to take place, although several Morris designs like the normal control LC3/4 were available with Austin badges through separate Austin dealers. In 1953, the LD-type 1-ton and 1½-ton vans were manufactured to a design that was finalised before the merger negotiations. Production continued until 1968, when it was replaced by the BMC EA.

Adderley Park seems to have ceased building forward control heavy lorries in 1955, with Austin at Longbridge taking over (including the Morris versions) until the opening of Bathgate, West Lothian in 1960. The LC3/4 was replaced that same year by the FG and FM, which were also offered as Austins, but production then moved to Bathgate in 1962.

In 1968, the Austin and Morris names were dropped, both becoming BMC for two years. The British Motor Corporation and Leyland Motors Ltd merged in 1968 to form the British Leyland Motor Corporation Ltd. Consequently, in 1970, any former BMC vehicles built at Bathgate were rebadged as 'Leyland', including the FG and WF normal control lorries.

Left: Morris Commercial Cars at Adderley Park, Birmingham was busy during World War 2 with military contracts. In 1948 it launched the Morris-Commercial FV lorry in the 5-ton forward control sector. However it had a decidedly pre-war look about it, particularly with its rear-hinged 'suicide' doors. This dropside lorry was photographed in early 1948.
Morris Motors

Above: This FV has a Scammell fifth wheel. It was photographed for this spring 1949 shot outside the Morris Motors Cowley plant with a load of four Minors for export, and was operated by vehicle delivery specialists B. J. Henry Ltd of Oxford. *Nuffield Organisation*

Right: The Morris-Commercial LC4 traced its origins to the pre-World War 2 LC 25/30-cwt vans and trucks and was a greatly improved version of the post-war LC3. It had an all-steel cab with a double-skinned roof and was available as a chassis-scuttle, chassis with cab or with an Anthony Hoist all-steel pick-up body, as seen here. When BMC was formed in 1952, the third-generation 30-cwt LC4 was launched. About a year later it was superseded by the 30-cwt LC5, which was joined in 1954 by the diesel-engined LC05. In 1954, these were rebadged as Morris and joined by Austin-badged versions. *Nuffield Organisation*

Above: This view is of Morris-Commercial vehicles at the 1953 Scottish Motor Show and shows the FV Series II cab with narrower, front-hinged doors. There were both Morris and Austin versions: the Morris had this distinctive inverted heart-shaped grille on the Willenhall cab, also seen on the initial versions of the J Type and LD vans, while the Austin cabs had a low-mounted horizontal grille. This new diesel-engined dray was No 114 in the William Younger & Co Ltd fleet. *Ian Allan Library*

Left: In 1955, the FV was replaced by the FE (Series III) cab. The individual Morris and Austin styling was substituted by a single corporate emblem, although it was still sold by both dealership chains. It was also adopted for a subsequent 7-ton version, although this was badged in theory only as a BMC. This official shot of a diesel-engined FE 7-ton tipper chassis cab is from September 1956 and has a Morris badge, so it may have been a preproduction vehicle. The new swb (10ft) lorry was available for a 6 cu yd capacity body. The price was £1,638 16s 2d. *Ian Allan Library*

Right: This January 1957 shot is of the first Morris FE artic to join the fleet of T. Wall & Son (Ice Cream) Ltd of West London, Manchester and Edinburgh. The outfit had a 23ft chassis, weighed 10 tons and carried 2,400 gallons of ice cream. The cab had a radio and heater, and there was a special compartment for cans of wafer biscuits outside the insulated vehicle body. As with other Wall's vehicles, it was bodied by Hooper & Co (Coachbuilders) Ltd.
Ian Allan Library

Right: The new FG truck was introduced in time for 1960, with payload ratings ranging from 1½-5 tons. It would replace the lower end of the forward control FE range. The 'threepenny bit' cab on this late-1959 diesel-engined 1½-tonner had what were described as 'angle-planned' doors that would make reversing 'child's play' and permit a generous field of vision to the rear. The FG (and 'snout-nosed' FM from 1961-78) was also sold as an Austin, then as a BMC from 1968-70, and finally as a Leyland until the early 1980s. Production of FG and FM lorries moved to Bathgate, Scotland in 1963.
Ian Allan Library

Left: The 1958-61 Morris FF was also sold as the Austin 45 and was intended to replace the upper end of the FE range. The FF came in 5, 7 and 8-ton variations. This apparently petrol-engined 1959 FF has 'BMC' as part of the Morris badge. It was in service with National Benzole, by then part of Shell-Mex & BP Ltd. The similar-looking FH replaced the FF in 1961 and was itself replaced in 1964. *Ian Allan Library*

Below: Passing over Westminster Bridge in 1965 is this 1963-registered Morris FG with the longer BMC diesel engine (hence the grille design). *Ian Allan Library*

Above This June 1963 official photograph is of a Morris FG K100 5-ton low-loading lorry with BMC FG safety cab and Hiab speed loader by the George Cohen 600 Group Ltd.
Ian Allan Library

Right: From 1964, the Morris Bathgate-built FJ was also sold as the Austin FJ. The all-new tilt cab was introduced to replace the FH range. The FJ was available with Morris and Austin badges with non-HGV ratings of 5 tons (K100) and 7 tons (K140). The heavier 8-ton K160 and 10-ton K360 Prime Mover were badged as BMC.
Ian Allan Library

Left: This was the ninth Bonallack 1240 cu ft-capacity light-alloy Luton-bodied Morris 5-ton FJ K100 supplied to Brocklehurst Yarns Ltd of Cardiff by City Commercials (Cardiff) Ltd. They were used to distribute to customers throughout the UK. The plywood floor and lower half of the Luton front were hinged to allow the cab to tilt forward. The FJ became the BMC Pilot cab in 1968. *Bonallack & Sons*

Left: The Post Office was always a big Morris fleet operator (including most FMs) and commissioned a number of these FG-based Luton-style vans for various departments during the 1960s. *Ian Allan Library*

PROCTOR

1946-52

Haulier Proctor Springwood Ltd of Mousehold, Norwich, was founded in the 1930s. Keen to improve the performance of its fleet, after World War 2 it built a prototype 6-ton lorry using proprietary components, including a Perkins P6 engine with a Moss gearbox and rear axle. A swb dump truck and tractor unit were then added to the range, all badged as 'Proctor'. In 1949, the distributor Praill's of Hereford took over production, resulting in the BRS Hereford branch making a number of Proctor lorries. Others were transferred from other branches and it became a Proctor 'hot spot', along with Hoover in Merthyr Tydfil which had the largest fleet. Production ceased in 1952.

Right: A Proctor tractor unit at the 1948 Commercial Vehicle Show, before Praill's of Hereford took over production. *CHC aau262*

Below: This is believed to be the post-war prototype, tested here by *Commercial Motor*, as it carries a Norfolk trade plate. *CHC aay248*

Below right: A very wintry scene with a Hereford-built lorry on test with *Commercial Motor*, just before production ended. *CHC aax198*

ROTINOFF

1952-62

George Rotinoff, son of a Russian engineer, set up Rotinoff Motors Ltd at Colnbrook near Slough, Buckinghamshire in 1952, to build heavy haulage tractors suitable for military tank transport. After suitability trials, the 6x4 Rotinoff Atlantic GR7 was approved by the Swiss Army, which purchased 12 for pulling tank transporters. Only one vehicle was sold new in the UK, to heavy-haulage operator Sunter Bros of Northallerton. Later, several were re-imported into the UK and sold on by dealers Walkers Machinery of Oxford.

The range included a number of different models. The Rotinoff Atlantic GR7, a 6x4 140-ton gross 250bhp tractor, was powered by a six-cylinder supercharged Rolls-Royce C6.SFL engine, with a David Brown 12-speed gearbox and Kirkstall rear bogie with twin axles. Later models had the 275bhp C6.TFL Rolls-Royce turbocharged diesel engine and 15-speed transmission. The Rotinoff Super Atlantic, a 6x4 330-ton gross 366bhp tractor, was powered by an eight-cylinder Rolls Royce C8.SFL engine, with a 15 or 18-speed gearbox. The Rotinoff Viscount 64.GKS was a smaller model, two of the 24ft lwb tractors sold to Vestey Brothers for Australian cattle roadtrain operations. Also listed was a forward control Viscount 84.BJS Rigid 8 drawbar tractor and the Rotinoff Pacific, a heavy-duty Dumper, of which one prototype is believed to have been built.

George Rotinoff died in 1959, when a total of only 35 vehicles had been built bearing his name. From 1960, the company changed its name to Lomount Vehicles & Engineering Ltd, which produced an Atlantic and Super Atlantic tank-transporter brochure entitled Lomount Heavy Vehicles. In 1962, the design rights were acquired by Atkinson Vehicles Ltd, which briefly marketed the trucks as 'Atkinsons', the brochures showing Atlantics with the 'A' radiator badge (though none appear to have actually been built). Atkinson had bought up the Rotinoff spares, stock and designs and appeared to be planning production of Rotinoff-type prime movers, but had already launched its Omega oilfield tractors in 1957 with Rolls-Royce engines.

Below: This is Rotinoff Motors Ltd's 1955-registered Atlantic demonstration vehicle, photographed by *Commercial Motor* while on test in Surrey with a trailer and tank. The 'GR' is a spoof military emblem, possibly a divided blue/yellow Royal Army Service Corps legend with George Rotinoffs's initials superimposed. The tank is a Centurion and may well have been a prototype ('P15' is written on the turret), which would suggest it was from the Fighting Vehicle Research and Development Establishment (FVRDE) at Chertsey, Surrey. Alternatively it may have been one of the several tanks Rotinoff sold for further use as tracked vehicles. The demonstrator had left-hand drive configuration to interest overseas customers, outside of those Commonwealth countries which mainly drove on the left.
CHC 00575

ROWE

Rowe Hillmaster was a commercial vehicle manufacturer founded in 1953 by local coach and garage operator Maurice G. Rowe of Rowe's Garage Ltd (itself founded in 1946) of Dobwalls, Liskeard in Cornwall. Having visited the 1952 Earls Court Commercial Motor Show and taken an instant liking to the new Meadows 4DC engine, he had one delivered and immediately set to work designing a chassis around it. As five coaches were built from 1953-58, the manufacturing side of the business became M. G. Rowe (Motors) Doublebois Ltd.

The first vehicles to come out of the Dobwalls workshop featured the relatively new four-cylinder 5.4-litre Meadows engine, which founder Maurice Rowe and engineer Wilfred Yeo had modified to run on its side, thus fitting under the floor. Although Meadows insisted it could not be done, after seeing the working example in the Dobwalls workshop the company was so impressed that, following further collaboration, the horizontal engine went into production, with the designation '4HDC'. The Rowe Hillmaster coach was the first application of a Meadows engine in a chassis design from the outset. The company then moved into commercial vehicle building, once again under the Hillmaster name, in 1954.

They were custom-built vehicles, produced specifically for use in the West Country. Being very adaptable, however, they soon became a fairly common sight on British roads, while a number were exported to Spain, Canada and New Zealand.

Cornwall's roads are different from most others in Britain, due to the very nature of the county. It is only just over 40 miles across at its widest, on the 'eastern frontier' with the rest of England. In such a confined place, the roads tend to be very narrow and also very hilly.

To get the optimum performance from any vehicle, it needs to have the right specification. It was with this in mind that the Rowe Hillmasters were built. They were narrower than most commercial vehicles, weighed less and had the correct gearing for West Country roads. These lorries and buses were built to suit customers' needs – literally 'custom-built'.

The trucks ranged from six to 14-ton payloads, in standard form, and a 15-ton articulated tractor unit. The cabs were supplied by coachbuilders Jennings, of Sandbach in Cheshire, and consequently appeared similar to ERFs of the period. Sales were limited and production would cease in 1962, after building 125 vehicles.

Above: A Hillmaster tipper parked in Bowling Green Lane in Central London in the late 1950s. It was evidently running on Rowe's trade plates and was driven up for testing. *CHC aar180*

Left: This 10-ton Hillmaster articulated tractor is seen on test with a dropside single-axle trailer. Note the lack of any other traffic. *CHC aae592*

Above: One of the commercial vehicle magazines tested this Hillmaster 7-ton dropside demonstrator. Note the emphasis on the underfloor engine. *CHC aav544*

Left: A view of a 7-tonner Hillmaster chassis. *Ian Allan Library*

Below: This Hillmaster was registered in Nottinghamshire in spring 1961, not long before production ended. It was photographed in Leicester around 1962. *CHC aah742*

SCAMMELL

The name 'Scammell' is automatically associated with articulated lorries, mechanical horses and heavy haulage. Scammell & Nephew started business as a wheelwright and coachbuilder, before producing its articulated lorry in 1919, utilising experience gained in World War 1.

As a result, Scammell Lorries Ltd was founded in 1922 and began producing articulated tanker vehicles. In the late 1920s, the first of a long line of rugged tractor units appeared which were especially designed for the haulage of heavy, out-of-gauge loads. In 1931, rigid six-wheelers were also added to the range, followed by the Rigid 8 by the end of the 1930s.

Scammell became well-known from 1933 for the design and production of its Mechanical Horse, updated in design in 1945 as the Scarab and continued in production until the 1960s – by which time the Townsman version acquired a glass-fibre cab, after a four-wheeled version with a Standard Atlas cab was still-born.

During World War 2, Scammell produced the 6x6 Pioneer used for tank transporters, recovery vehicles and artillery tractors, or later by showmen and recovery operators when they were sold off by the War Department. Scammell also produced a large number of heavy-duty trailer fire pumps.

In 1949/50, the 4x4 Mountaineer was designed for civilian use, based in part on the military Pioneer. Production of a well-designed range of rigids and tractor units continued during the next six years but, in 1955, Scammell was bought out by Leyland, which wisely kept the Watford plant in operation without any drastic changes.

The bonneted articulated tractor continued to be offered and was updated in the late 1950s as the Highwayman, re-rated at 24 tons gcw, though in practice much higher weights were often handled. The Mountaineer was joined in 1952 by the 6x6 Constructor with Rolls-Royce engine, which found favour in the desert oilfields and also in the domestic heavy haulage market as a 100-ton tractor. This was later joined by the 6x4 Junior Constructor, as well as the uprated Super Constructor. Once again, this was later upstaged by the Contractor, which reverted to a 6x4 configuration

Left: The 3-ton and 6-ton Mechanical Horse range continued to be produced after World War 2, albeit to the pre-war designs. Many pre-war tractors continued in service, often for many years. This Mechanical Horse was in the service of W. H. Smith & Sons of Boston, Lincolnshire, and was photographed in the 1950s. *CHC aaz632*

with Rolls-Royce or Cummins power and Self-Changing Gears automatic gearbox, available with rated capacities of 125-240 tons (although capable of much more).

Meanwhile, in 1960 the Handyman made its appearance, modified in 1964 with a Michelotti-designed cab also fitted to the rigid eight-wheeled 24-ton gvw Routeman which first appeared in 1960, the same year the Trunker 6x2 tractor unit entered production (also updated in 1964).

In 1970, the Crusader 4x2 tractor was introduced, largely to fulfill the requirements of BRS, which took a large part of the production output over the next 10 years, though it was not widely used by other hauliers. A 6x4 version was used by the military in various roles, including recovery vehicles and tank transporters, as well as some heavy hauliers like Wynns and Pickfords.

Prior to the closure of AEC's works, AEC Southall built Marathons from 1973 until April 1979. 60 Marathons were also built by Guy. Marathon production was transferred to Watford in May 1979 but ended in December 1980, by which time another 670 had been built.

Until the late 1980s, Scammell remained the specialised vehicles division of Leyland, producing heavy tractors and, since the 1970s, former Thornycroft models such as the Nubian airport firefighting vehicle and the Amazon 6x6 tractor for gross weights up to 300 tons, now fitted with the Leyland cab similar to the Landtrain series. Other contemporary models included the Constructor and S26, covering a range from 24-300 tonnes gcw, both of which featured the Leyland C40 cab.

In February 1987, Scammell learned that its tender for 1,522 military vehicles for the Ministry of Defence was successful. Although designed by Scammell (which also designed the Constructor eight-wheelers), the four-axled D.R.O.P.S. (Demonstrable Rack Offload and Pickup System) vehicles were in fact built at the Leyland Assembly Plant (LAP) as originally intended. After the Leyland group was purchased by DAF BV of Holland, assembly of selected S26 models was transferred to the Leyland plant in Lancashire. The Watford factory closed – and that was the end of the Scammell name.

However, this was not the end of the story. Upon closure in July 1988, the S24 and the Nubian ranges, together with rights to the Crusader and Commander, were bought by Unipower Ltd which opened a new plant in West Watford. This company also provided continuing support for Scammell lorries.

In the 1980s, Unipower launched the C Series heavy-haulage tractor and a range of military lorries. Alvis plc acquired the company in 1994 and named their new subsidiary Alvis Unipower Limited, which is how the trucks began to be branded.

Following its elimination from the bidding process for the MoD's Heavy Equipment Transporter (HET) project, Alvis announced in 1999 its intention to seek a new owner for Alvis Unipower. This was unsuccessful. The prototypes built for this contract were subsequently sold to Abnormal Load Engineering (ALE) of Stafford, which specialises in moving items like turbines and transformers for the power industry, for use as heavy-haulage ballast tractors.

Right: The Mechanical Horse was replaced in 1948 by the Scarab, production of which continued until 1967. This shot dates from mid-1949 and is of a Corporation of London Scarab coupled to an 18 cu yd moving floor refuse collector trailer. *Ian Allan Library*

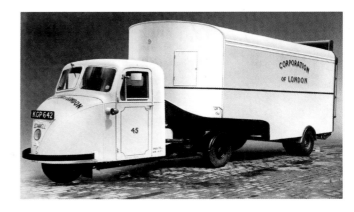

Below: State-owned haulier Pickfords purchased many Scammell tractors over the years. In this January 1956 view, the almost-new Constructor in front (No 8931) is towing a heavy six-axle trailer with another tractor pushing. The location is apparently Finsbury Market in London. *Ian Allan Library*

Right: This 15MU tractor unit and matching tank trailer were new in 1953. In this 1957 view they are at the Stratford, East London works of A. Boake Roberts & Co Ltd, about to be loaded with 3,600 gallons of chemicals. No 117m was one of 87 Scammell tractors and more than 100 semi-trailers operated by Crow Carrying Co Ltd of Barking, Essex. *Ian Allan Library*

Above: Hallett, Silbermann Ltd operated this Scammell Highwayman, as it became known, as a ballast tractor for the haulage of long and heavy loads. On the trailer and dolly is what appears to be an export railway car from D. Wickham & Co Ltd of Ware, Hertfordshire. *Ian Allan Library*

Above: This November 1963 view is of a later GRP-cabbed 30-ton Highwayman tractor and swan-neck trailer, which would be displayed at the Scammell stand during the 1963 Scottish Motor Exhibition. *Scammell Lorries*

Right: Scammell introduced the Handyman I in 1960 with its own design of GRP cab. Destined for Scottish haulier McKelvie, this model is seen at a commercial vehicle show. It was superseded after a couple of years by the Michelotti-designed ribbed-style cab for the Handyman, Routeman and Trunker. *CHC abj627*

Right: Geest Horticultural Products was established in 1935, to import bulbs from the Netherlands to their Spalding base. The company later started importing bananas in 1953 and then began a shipping and cruise line in 1959. This 1967 Lincolnshire-registered Handyman was part of the Geest fleet. In this August 1968 view, it is coupled to a trailer hauling four containers, presumably loaded with bulbs. *Ian Allan Library*

Right: This twin-steer Trunker is on a road test in late 1967, with a concrete test load on the two-axle platform trailer. The GRP cab was designed by Michelotti of Italy.
Ian Allan Library

Right: This November 1968 shot shows a six-wheeled twin-steer Trunker II tractor, designed to allow 32-ton operation on five axles with a tandem-axle trailer. It was fleet 166, coupled to tanker trailer T166, with United Molasses. *Scammell Lorries*

Above: Well-known heavy haulier Sunters Bros Ltd of Northallerton, North Yorkshire operated this 1970-registered Constructor, seen towing Duchess of Sutherland from Thetford to Bressingham Steam Museum through South Lopham, Norfolk, on 21 March 1971. *Ian Allan Library*

Below: Shell-Mex and BP Ltd was a long-time Scammell tractor user and this Trunker four-wheeler was No 74077 in its fleet, new in 1968. It is seen coupled to Thompson Bros (Bilston) Ltd tanker-trailer No 02371. *Thompson Bros*

Right: This 1978/9 view shows one of three 30-ton Routeman eight-wheeled chassis acquired by the Forestry Commission with extended wheelbases (to 21ft) and frames (by 5ft 7in). They were three out of the seven working in the Cannock, Delaware and Sherwood Forests that handled loads up to 18 tonnes, with loading/unloading by HIAB cranes. Two of the Routemans had Rolls-Royce Eagle Mk III engines (as here) and the third a Leyland T41, while all had David Brown eight-speed gearboxes. *Ian Allan Library*

Above: The Scammell S24 was introduced in 1980 and was the last to be developed before production ended in 1988. Its design was based on the varying military and civilian uses of the earlier Contractor models. In May 1988, Unipower Vehicles Ltd acquired the design, manufacturing and support rights for the Scammell S24 range. The S24 Contractor range was available in 6x4 and 6x6, rarely selling in 4x2 configurations. Both lhd and rhd were available. Cummins N & K in-line series and Perkins RF CV8 power units were used, the standard power unit being a 14-litre Cummins NTE-350, driving through a Spicer manual gearbox and Brockhouse torque converter (semiautomatic) or an Allison automatic transmission. Capacities were on/off road up to 150 tonnes gross and up to 300 tonnes on restricted applications. *Ian Allan Library*

Above: The Scammell S26 used the Leyland T45 Roadtrain cab to create a forward control heavy-haulage tractor, otherwise similar to the S24. An example of the S26, destined for the Wynns fleet, is seen at a show. *CHC abg799*

Above: This is an official shot by Leyland Vehicles (from 1978, the new name of the former Truck & Bus Division) of their new Commander tank-transporter tractor. The Commander had its origins in a British Army requirement that envisaged main battle tanks weighing well over 60 tonnes, and was originally developed to replace the old Thornycroft Antars. Although development began in 1976, production of the 125 units did not begin until 1983. The engine was a Perkins (Rolls-Royce) CV 12 TCE V12 turbocharged diesel driving through Allison automatic transmission, though other engines were also proposed (one prototype used a Cummins KTA 600 diesel). In 1988, the rights to the Commander were bought by Unipower Ltd, which opened a new plant in West Watford. *Leyland Vehicles*

Above: The 1966-8 Scammell Townsman three-wheeler replaced the 3-ton Scarab. The new GRP cab was accompanied by other improvements such as vacuum-assisted hydraulic brakes, a heater-demister, two rearview mirrors, interior sunvisors, totally enclosed oil-immersed coil-spring front suspension and dual-rate mounting of semi-elliptic leaf springs at the rear. The frame was a welded construction with integral coupling ramps fitted with Scammell Mechanical Horse automatic coupling. A vacuum-operated release mechanism replaced the Scarab's hand lever. The diesel engine, gearbox and driving axle formed a ridged assembly pivoted at the front end in a large rubber bush. This new tug was exhibited at a Commercial Motor Show in British Rail's yellow Railfreight livery. Some were also used by the General Post Office for Royal Mail work. *CHC aaa131*

Above: The Scarab-Four was intended to appeal mainly to operators of the successful three-wheeled Scarab. Leyland's acquisition of Standard in 1961 enabled Scammell's engineers to develop a tractor unit more suitable to longer-haul working. The idea was to combine the three-wheeled Scarab and the Standard Atlas van. The Atlas front end would provide a new and more comfortable cab with four wheels for longer journeys, while the Scarab's back end would provide interchangeability with existing fleets of trailers. The engine used was the Standard 2.26-litre diesel, which was mounted behind the cab though tilted at 50° to lower the height. It was announced at the 1962 Commercial Motor Show and production started in mid-1964 – by which time the Atlas had become the Leyland Fifteen and Twenty. However, fewer than 100 Scarab-Fours were produced, the majority going to South African Railways. *Roy Larkin*

SEDDON

1937-74

Foster and Seddon began commercial vehicle manufacturing in 1937, having previously been engaged in the distribution and repair of vehicles for 18 years. The company's first vehicle was a forward control lightweight 6-ton chassis, fitted with a Perkins P6 diesel engine. It was beginning to prove popular with operators when World War 2 called a halt to further production. After the war, the model reappeared and the firm became Seddon Lorries from 1947. The range was expanded and, in 1950, a smaller 3-ton lorry, the Mk 7, appeared, powered by a Perkins engine. Two years later, a normal control 25-30-cwt van known as the 25 range was produced, which incorporated many glass-fibre body panels. This was not particularly popular, although the three-tonner remained in production until 1963.

Styling changes took place in 1956, when the original Mk 5 was updated with wrap-around windscreens, while a year later some models became obtainable with plastic cab panels. Emphasis shifted to the heavier models in 1956/7, when a 14-ton gvw chassis known as the Mk 15 was put on the market, using a new-style plastics cab. Heavier rigids entered production in 1958, including the SD8 and DD8, Gardner-engined single and double-drive eight-wheelers. There were also tractor units like the Mk 8 and later heavier models.

From 1964 onwards, the Motor Panels cab was also fitted to the Guy Big J, Scammell Crusader and various other vehicles, appearing on all Seddon models. The model classification was complicated, based upon the gross weight, number of axles and engine type, and so the models ranged from the 12.4.354 for a Perkins-powered 12-tonner to the 32.4.240. In 1967, tractor units appeared for 28 tons or 32 tons gross, powered by Rolls-Royce or Gardener engines. Seddon also did well with chassis for the refuse collection vehicle market into the 1970s.

Seddon was able to take over the old, established firm of Atkinson in 1970 and, within two years, a new heavy range was designed. Both companies' models continued to be produced separately under the two names until, in 1974, the new concern was acquired by International Harvester and became Seddon Atkinson, with a completely new range.

Right: The lorry in front is a Mk V, basically the same vehicle that was offered from the pre-World War 2 period through until the mid-1950s. It was photographed at Oldham, about to be road tested by *Commercial Motor*. Seddon Motors Ltd continued in the post-war period to supply private users, though this market was affected by the 1948 nationalisation of road transport. *CHC aae286*

Above: Seddon Motors became Seddon Diesel Vehicles Ltd in 1950. This Birmingham-registered Seddon Mk 7 Luton van was new in early 1953 to Alfred Conner & Co Ltd of Nuneaton, which evidently recycled cardboard and paper into packaging materials. *Ian Allan Library*

Left: This shot dates from autumn 1955 and shows a tractor with haulage contractors P. A. Carter & Sons Ltd of London SE10 and Wolverhampton. It was supplied by Halls (Finchley) Ltd of north London and featured the new wide-vision cab. *Godwin*

Right: A Seddon tipper photographed in 1956 in Campbell's stone quarry near Salisbury, Rhodesia (now Harare, Zimbabwe). It had the Perkins P6(V) engine and was operated by Red Line Transport and Warehouse Co (PVT) Ltd. *F. Perkins Ltd*

Right: This November 1957 shot is of a Mk 15 chassis-cab running at 11 tons gvw. It was fitted with a Perkins P6 engine. The Mk 15 was first introduced at the 1956 London Commercial Motor Show, by which time Seddon vehicles were operating in Belgium, the Netherlands, Cyprus, Thailand, South America, South Africa, Rhodesia, Portugal, Spain and Jamaica. *Mack of Manchester*

Right: Hauliers I. Scarr & Sons of Selby (then in West Riding), Yorkshire operated this DD8 double-drive eight-wheeled dropside when photographed in the summer of 1959. *Mack of Manchester*

Left: This model 13:Four was one of two supplied in November 1965 to Waterhouse Animal Feeds with a 600 cu ft double-skinned tipping alloy body by Spencer (Melksham) Ltd. It was used to convey bulk grain and animal foodstuffs and had a 14ft 8in wheelbase. *Mack of Manchester*

Below: This 1965-registered 30-4-6LX tractor – the AEC badge probably signifying the engine manufacturer – was No 315 with the BRS Roadferry subsidiary. It was photographed in 1966 at Immingham, having just picked up a trailer off the Tor Line Ro-Ro vessel Tor Anglia, registered in Gothenburg. *Ian Allan Library*

Right: H. G. Blake (Costessey) Ltd (farmers and wholesale butchers based in Costessey, near Norwich) operated this 1968-registered six-wheeler, with the Motor Panels cab used on all Seddons by this time and an insulated refrigerated van body. *Seddon Motors*

Below: In this August 1968 photograph, a Chichester Rural District Council (Sussex) model 16:Four 28-ton gross tractor is coupled to a 4,000-gallon Vacuum Cesspit Emptier mounted on a frameless semitrailer. Its total length was 32ft 3in; the tank section was built by Eagle Engineering Co Ltd of Warwick, with an exhauster pump driven off the tractor. Similar 32-ton tractor units were popular with BRS. *Ian Allan Library*

SEDDON ATKINSON

1974-2004

The American corporation International Harvester already had a European interest in commercial vehicles, having acquired a stake in the Dutch company DAF. It had also made a similar small effort in the UK in the years 1965-69.

When Seddon Atkinson was acquired in 1974, the range was already well established and continued unaltered, in spite of rumours that all models would have the same cab design as DAF. In 1975, the new 400 range of heavyweight four, six and eight-wheeled rigids were in production, as well as a 4x2 articulated tractor unit for 32 tons gcw. One year later a lighter four-wheel rigid for 17 tons gross was offered, designated the 200 series and powered by the International D358 engine. The 300 series appeared in 1978, which was a six-wheeled rigid for 24 tons gvw. In 1982, the 200, 300 and 400 series were superseded by the similar but improved 201, 301 and 401 respectively.

International Harvester also had shares in ENASA, a Spanish-owned vehicle manufacturer, and, when the US company suffered severe financial difficulties in the 1980s, several of its overseas subsidiaries were sold off. Seddon Atkinson was sold to ENASA in 1984, which was now independent of the Americans.

The 201, 301 and 401 ranges from 1981/2 continued into the mid-1980s with minor improvements, differing engine options and additional models, like the 301 lightweight tractor unit. The cab interiors were also modified and the gearbox linkage improved. In 1986, these were replaced by the 2-11, 3-11 and 4-11 models. The Motor Panels cab retained basically the same design which had first appeared in 1975.

Below: Seddon Atkinson Vehicles Ltd was formed on the acquisition of Atkinson Vehicles of Preston in 1970 by Seddon Diesel Vehicles of Oldham. In 1974, the firm was acquired by the American giant International Harvester. In this April 1977 photograph, three new Seddon Atkinsons had been put into service with Danepak Ltd of Thetford, supplied by J. F. Duffield Ltd of Norwich: a 400 Series tractor (left) and two 16-tonne 200 Series rigids. They had Freight Bonallack Coldsaver refrigerated bodies and were used for the nationwide delivery of bacon. The 200 Series had International D-358 diesel engines with Eaton five-speed gearboxes and 89120 rear axles. The Preston-assembled 400 Series had a Gardner 8LXB driving through a Fuller five-speed gearbox and SA-13-HR rear axle. *B. J. Rampley*

For a time, the 2-11 chassis also formed the basis of a refuse collection vehicle sold by Jack Allen, the Birmingham-based specialist in this market. This was the Britannia, fitted with a low-entry crew cab supplied by Walter Alexander, the Falkirk-based bus bodybuilder.

From 1988, the 4-11 and 3-11 were replaced by a new family of trucks, starting with the Strato tractor unit. The latter was fitted with a cab developed by Cabtec, a joint venture between ENASA and DAF, which was also used on the DAF 95 and ENASA's Pegaso Troner and was available briefly in the UK through Seddon Atkinson dealers.

There was another, more dramatic change of ownership at Seddon Atkinson in 1991, when Iveco bought the Spanish Government's stake in ENASA's truck and bus-building businesses.

It seems that Seddon Atkinson was not part of the grand Iveco plan, but came with the Spanish operation. After a delay while the new owner came to terms with its new British acquisition, it began to be integrated into Iveco's European operations. The big difference was that Seddon Atkinson used bought-in engines while Iveco, as a vertically integrated company, made its own engines or had a financial interest in the companies making them.

In 1992, the 2-11 was replaced by the Strato 210, a Perkins-engined chassis with the then new Iveco Euro cab also fitted on the Iveco Cargo (see Ford chapter, page 86). The heavier models were fitted with the wider version of the Euro cab instead of the Cabtec product, which was discontinued. Most models continued to be built with large grilles adorned with the Seddon Atkinson name and the distinctive encircled 'A' logo dating back to Atkinson days, although some refuse collection vehicles were fitted with Iveco grilles.

In 1997, Seddon Atkinson produced the Leader, a revolutionary refuse collection chassis that also had potential as an Iveco product. The driveline of this four- and six-wheel chassis was fairly conventional, with a Cummins C series engine and Allison automatic gearbox, but it featured a highly distinctive cab with a central driving position to allow more room for the crew.

In 2004, the Oldham factory closed when production moved to Iveco's factory in Madrid, Spain. In June 2006, Iveco announced that, as from the introduction of Euro-4 in October, Seddon Atkinson vehicles would no longer be produced. Due to the prohibitive cost of redesigning the refuse vehicle, Iveco was withdrawing from the manufacture of low-entry refuse trucks.

Above: In March 1978, Storage and Haulage Ltd of Birmingham had just put into service five 14ft 8in wheelbase 200 Series drawbar outfits with York drawbar trailers, supplied by Scott's Commercial Vehicles of Earl Shilton. They were used on contract to Kellogg's and operated out of a Hatfield, Hertfordshire warehouse, delivering cereals around the country. With a ulw of 8 tons 17-cwt, they could carry a payload of 9-9½ tons within the plated weight of 20 tons gross. *Martin Coombes AIIP Ltd*

Left: M. Woodhouse (Transport) Ltd is still based in Halton, Lancaster. New in 1978, the company's No 7 was a 400 Series Tractor, named Jillian, used for bulk haulage with a Lancaster Transport (part of the MW Group) tipping trailer. *Ian Allan Library*

Right: Haulage contractor Frederick Ray Ltd of Leighton Buzzard, Bedfordshire operated this Seddon Atkinson 400 tractor as its No 242. *Kevin Lane*

Left: The traditional Atkinson 'A' returned to the radiator, as shown by this new 401 model tractor. The Atkinson works assembled the 400 series and also the first batch of the new 401 model, before closing at the end of 1981. Production then moved to Oldham. The 401 parts list suggests that the vehicle had a Cummins 320 engine and Fuller 11609 gearbox, while another source suggests a nine-speed Roadranger gearbox.
Ian Allan Library

Left: The 300 tractor was apparently not too successful with its International DTi 466 engine, but when it was reintroduced around 1982 as the 301, with Cummins L10 engine (and 'A' radiator badge), it proved popular. In February 1983, Seddon Atkinson was purchased by the Spanish group ENASA, which made it a subsidiary of Pegaso, a manufacturer of medium-sized commercial vehicles. When this photograph was taken, the 4x2 and 6x2 tractors carried SST8010 transmissions and heavy duty driveshafts as standard. *Ian Allan Library*

Below: The last Seddon Atkinsons built before the IVECO takeover included the Strato tractor unit, which used a cab produced by Cabtec – a joint venture between ENASA and DAF, also seen then on the Pegaso Troner and DAF 95. This Strato was in the fleet of well-known haulier Eddie Stobart. *PM Photography*

Sentinel/TVW

The Scottish engineering firm of Alley and McLellan established the Sentinel steam waggon (always with a double 'g') in 1906, moving from Polmadie, Glasgow to Shrewsbury in 1918. Sentinels were popular and, by the mid-1920s, the company was producing a six-wheeler capable of a 15-ton payload. By the 1930s, the vehicles had modern equipment such as electric speedometers, electric lights, power take-off and self-stroking boilers. Their speed and absence of noise was quite remarkable, but steam lorries suffered from punitive taxation because of their high ulw.

During World War 2, the firm was prominent in experimentation and the manufacture of gas-producer trailers to help overcome the diesel and petrol shortage. The last steam waggons were produced as late as 1949 as an export order for Argentina, the UK market having fallen since the late 1930s.

Right: In 1947, Sentinel Waggon Works (1920) Ltd became Sentinel Ltd, based in Shrewsbury, Shropshire and with a central London office at Victoria Station House. The company introduced a new range of diesel lorries using its own four-cylinder diesel engine. This rigid brewery dray was new to Wilson's Brewery Ltd of Manchester in 1951 as No 21, though this shot is dated September 1952. Note the wide windscreen and radiator grille, plus the rear-hinging doors. *West Midlands Photo Services*

Right: This view of the chassis assembly area shows both lwb and swb four-wheeled and six-wheeled chassis cabs behind the bus underframe in the foreground. The Sentinel four-cylinder engine produced 90bhp at 2000 rpm, and there was also a six-cylinder. Despite Sentinel's engineering, sales diminished throughout the 1950s and, by 1956, the company was forced to cease lorry production. *Rooster Publicity Ltd*

Left: After Sentinel ceased assembly of lorries, its main agent, North Cheshire Motors Ltd, set up its own company, Transport Vehicles (Warrington) Ltd, in 1957, using Sentinel's designs but badged as 'TVW'. This is a Sentinel Light Six six-wheeled rigid, as supplied by North Cheshire Motors of Warrington. *CHC aar119*

Below: A view of the TVW works, with a six-wheeled chassis cab and at least two 4x2 tractors. *CHC aax315*

The Sentinel Waggon Works (1920) Ltd of Shrewsbury, Shropshire, became Sentinel (Shrewsbury) Ltd in 1946, having accepted that diesel trucks were the future. The company's first effort was the DV44 four-wheeler, which became available in 1948. A lightweight six-wheeled version, the DV46, soon followed, with the same four-cylinder six-litre Sentinel diesel of 90bhp. The DV66 six-wheeler with six cylinder engine appeared in 1952. Sentinels were fitted with a distinctive cab with sliding doors, but the most unusual feature was that the engine was positioned horizontally between the chassis rails behind the cab.

There were surprisingly few customers for these advanced diesel lorries and, in 1956, the company decided to cease production. The factory passed to Rolls-Royce for diesel-engine production. The last batch of vehicles, built after the Rolls-Royce takeover, was made up of aircraft tugs completed for the RAF.

After Sentinel ceased lorry production, the company's main agent, North Cheshire Motors Ltd, purchased the remaining stocks of vehicles and parts and set up its own company, Transport Vehicles (Warrington) Ltd in 1957, to build its own TVW lorries using Sentinel's designs. Most sales went to a group of former Sentinel customers who financially supported the venture. Best-selling products included an eight-wheel platform vehicle and a 24-ton gcw tractor unit. The company closed in 1961, having built about 100 trucks.

Right: This completed TVW six-wheeler chassis-cab is ready for delivery in primer. There was also an eight-wheeled chassis available under the TVW name. In 1961 the company closed, having built about 100 trucks.
CHC aax316

Below: This 1960-registered tipper was one of several lorries that included Sentinels and six-wheeled TVMs, photographed by *Commercial Motor* on a visit to A. Fletcher & Co Ltd of the coal-mining community of Ibstock, Leicestershire.
CHT aay294

SHELVOKE & DREWRY

1922-91

Shelvoke & Drewry Ltd was founded in 1922 in Letchworth, Hertfordshire by Harry Shelvoke and James Drewry, both of whom had successful careers in commercial vehicle design and manufacture. Prior to World War 2, the main vehicle produced was the tiller-steered Freighter for the municipal market, of which there was a number produced up to 1952. During the period 1939-45, the company's entire output was devoted to the war effort. Post-war, a new design known as the W-type, which offered a higher capacity on a conventional-style chassis, was tested and demonstrated in the severe winter of 1946/7, immediately finding favour with the municipal councils. An updated version of the pre-war 'Fore & Aft' Tipper was designed and also proved popular.

By 1959, the new regulations permitted a gross weight of 14 tons, but the gross weight of the W type was only 8 tons 11-cwt. Clearly, there was a need for a replacement vehicle. The T type was designed in August 1959 and the prototype was on test by the autumn.

A further factory was built in Blackhorse Road, Letchworth, for the construction of these new models. In 1969, the Paka Ejector model was introduced to overcome the problems of tipping on rough dumps, which could make the vehicle unstable or cause the body to distort.

In 1971, the Revopak was introduced with continuously rotating tines which were able to break up items like discarded cookers or fridges with ease. The NY series of 1972 introduced all-steel cabs from Motor Panels Ltd, and, by 1975, 650 NXs had been produced and 1,700 NYs. The smallest N-type, the NN, continued to use a version of the glass-fibre panelled cab of the T series.

SD had always made other types of vehicle, like heavy-duty forklifts, but from 1975 the company went head-to-head with arch-rival Dennis, manufacturing fire engines through its newly-established Special Purpose Vehicles (SPV) division. The chassis was also used for other specialised vehicles, for example in airport services.

The year 1978 saw the introduction of the P Series chassis. In January 1980, the 25,000 SD vehicle was completed – a 16-ton PY Series Revopak. However, by 1986 the company was known as Shelvoke Dempster, having become part of the US Dempster Brothers group. Its product range diversified further into front-end loading dustcarts (based on Dempster's ubiquitous Dumpster system), as well as a licence-built version of Dempster's Routechief rear-loading refuse body.

This did not prevent the company plunging deeper into financial crisis and, by the end of the 1980s, Dempster had pulled out. The remainder of the company was then absorbed into Dennis and the Dennis-Shelvoke name continued briefly, until the company closed down by the end of 1991.

Left: This Shelvoke & Drewry W-type refuse-collection vehicle was new in 1955 to Birmingham City Council, fitted with a 'Fore & Aft' tipping body for both compaction and unloading.
CHC aar555

Right: This shot was taken in 1979 and shows a Shelvoke & Drewry T-type refuse collection vehicle in service with the London Borough of Barnet. It is seen discharging its load at a highly-automated Greater London Council plant, where there were up to 300 daily arrivals. *GLC*

Below: Shelvoke & Drewry's SPV (Special Purposes Vehicles) was formed in 1975 and mainly produced fire appliances. However, there were also aircraft loaders, as with this 1980 15-ton gvw vehicle in the service of caterers Trusthouse Forte, seen at Heathrow Airport. It had a Norcolift Universal lifting mechanism, a Perkins diesel engine and the three-man cab was mounted on a drop-front chassis frame, with only 6ft to the top of the cab. *Ian Allan Library*

THORNYCROFT

1896-1962

In 1864, John Isaac Thornycroft began building steam-driven launches for river work. He later turned his attention to steam-driven road vehicles and, in 1896, produced a steam van, although he retained his marine interests. Early experiments with petrol and paraffin engines kept Thornycroft at the forefront of engineering and its J Type lorries of World War 1 fame continued to be built for civilian use some years after.

During the 1930s, Thornycroft made vehicles from 2-15 tons for a wide variety of uses, which were extremely popular with operators both large and small. It also produced some vehicles for specialised work, with the War Department ordering some 5,000 vehicles during World War 2 including the 4x4 Nubian and, later, the 6x4 Amazon model.

In 1948, the range comprised the 3-ton Nippy, 5/6-ton Sturdy, 8-ton Sturdy tractor, Amazon 12-ton six-wheeler and Trusty 15-ton eight-wheeler. In 1950, the 12-ton Trident rigid vehicle was introduced and the Sturdy revamped (now called the Sturdy Star, the word 'Star' also being applied to the Nippy model). Shortly after this, a new pressed-steel cab was introduced for most vehicles in the range, produced by Motor Panels and shared with Guy Motors (although the two firms were not otherwise connected in any way). The Nippy Star was replaced by the Swift and the Sturdy Star by the Swiftsure in 1957, when the Mastiff four-wheeled rigid seven-tonner also appeared.

In 1959/60, an attractive new cab with well-rounded corner panels was put on the market, but, before these had a chance to become familiar, Transport Equipment (Thornycroft) Ltd (to give the company its full title) was taken over by AEC and the range trimmed down to the Nubian model and some special-purpose vehicles. Eight years later, the Basingstoke works was sold and all production transferred to Scammell at Watford.

Special mention must be made of the Mighty Antar and Big Ben units, produced during the 1950s for the haulage of indivisible loads. The Big Ben was designed for oilfield work, for large loads of up to a maximum gross weight of 40 tons using a new 11.33-litre oil engine developing 155bhp from its six cylinders. The Antar was used as a six-wheeled tractor, both as a military tank transporter and by heavy haulage operators for gross weights in excess of 100 tons.

Left: During World War 2, John I. Thornycroft & Company Ltd produced military and civilian vehicles. In 1948, to differentiate the vehicle division in Basingstoke, Hampshire from the marine division, Transport Equipment (Thornycroft) Ltd was incorporated as a subsidiary. Photographed just before the establishment of the new company, this 1947-registered Trusty diesel eight-wheeler was No 14 in the fleet of removal and transport contractor J. H. Kirkham Ltd of Blackpool.
John I. Thornycroft

Above: This shot was taken in 1948, showing one of a batch of Sturdy 13ft 4in-wheelbase diesel or oil-engined lorries operated by Permalite Ltd, East London, which made roofing felt, damp coursing and asphalt for roofing and floors. They had works-built cabs and dropside bodies with a strong headboard and had to weigh below 3 tons for taxation purposes.
John I. Thornycroft

Right: This shot is dated June 1949 and shows two new Sturdy lorries being handed over to Arthur Guinness, Son & Co Ltd, in the brewing company's very smart black and white livery. They were for use at the Park Royal, North-West London brewery, established in 1936.
John I. Thornycroft

Left: Cotton manufacturers E. Knowles (Todmorden) Ltd of West Riding, Yorkshire operated this Sturdy Star flatbed rigid, new in February 1952. Note the Motor Panels all-steel cab also used at that time on 'Thornycrofts'. *John I. Thornycroft*

Below: This May 1955 photograph is of a new Trident 9 cu yd end tipper on the latest 11ft 6in wheelbase chassis. The Butterley Co Ltd of Derbyshire had taken delivery for transporting gravel and sand. The ulw was 3 tons 18¾-cwt, and the body was manufactured by Challands Ross & Co Ltd, the Thornycroft distributor in Nottingham. *John I. Thornycroft*

Right: This Trident diesel tractor was new in 1954 to L&H Ltd of Frodsham, Cheshire. Its load of Shell X-100 motor-oil drums is in a five-deck semi-trailer from British Trailer Co Ltd of Trafford Park, Manchester. *British Trailer Co*

Below: One of a number of Swift 4-ton lorries with works-built alloy bodies and standard all-steel cab, supplied in January 1957 to Dan Jones & Sons of Forth, Glamorgan. The bodywork was to the customer's specification, including hinged sides and solid top with side curtains for protection of fruit and vegetables. *John I. Thornycroft*

Left: This Trusty VF or PK eight-wheeler was a 14-ton rigid. Note the new design of cab and the unusual bodywork with trestles for carrying long girders. *Transport Vehicles (Thornycroft) Ltd*

Below: In 1961, Thornycroft was taken over by AEC, with production limited to Nubians and Big Ben and Antar heavy tractors. ACV was then taken over by Leyland, who already had a specialist vehicle unit in Scammell, another manufacturer of large haulage vehicles. This Big Ben 6x4 was presumably intended for oil exploration work. *AEC Ltd*

TROJAN

Originally designed by L. H. Hounsfield and built by Leyland at its Kingston works from 1924, with solid tyres and a 10hp two-stroke engine, the first commercial model had a carrying capacity of only 5-cwt (later uprated to 7-cwt). Production of all vehicles was transferred to the enlarged Purley Way, Croydon factory and car production ceased. A 10-cwt version, basically similar to the 7-cwt model, appeared in 1930 and remained in production until 1942. Trojan then ceased vehicle production and produced precision engineering components and munitions for the war effort.

Trojan's vehicles were popular with local tradesmen, but were extensively used by the Brooke Bond Tea Co of Manchester and Croydon. From 1947, a completely new design for a medium-sized 15-cwt van was drawn up with a conventional chassis and shaft drive through a normal gearbox. At first these vans used a modified version of the original two-stroke engine design, which had been given two extra cylinders on the side of the block to act as injector pumps for the fuel. Though this method worked quite well, fuel consumption was rather heavy and a three-cylinder Perkins P3V diesel engine was substituted in 1951.

This model was produced in various forms including personnel carriers, dropside trucks and even an articulated version, as well as the normal and forward control one-ton vans. The last model was introduced in 1958 as a forward control 25-cwt with Perkins engine. From around 1960, the Trojan factory was used to assemble Lambretta scooters for the English market.

Above: Trojan Ltd of Croydon, Surrey produced vans until the outbreak of World War 2. After the war, production restarted in 1946 (still with the original engine until 1952), though full production was not reached until 1948. The '15', a 5-cwt commercial, used a 2.3-litre 24bhp two-stroke Trojan '65' four-cylinder engine. Trojan had agents overseas in the Netherlands, Portugal, Sweden, Denmark, Norway, Australia, New Zealand and Ireland. This official shot is dated December 1947 and was evidently taken at the Croydon works. *Ian Allan Library*

Left: Trojan were the first manufacturer to use diesel engines in a one-ton (actually 25-cwt) van. Trojan offered an articulated version as well, as illustrated here. This mini-artic was coupled to a Taskers van trailer. *Ian Allan Library*

Left: In 1952, the more efficient and powerful Perkins P3V three-cylinder diesel engine replaced the Trojan engine in the new range of normal control vehicles. This is a 25-cwt truck on the Trojan stand, probably photographed at the 1952 London *Commercial Motor* Show. In 1952, the Trojan design style had changed from round wings with headlights on top to square wings with integral headlights. *CHC aar080*

Left: Trojan continued to produce custom bodies, with all-steel bodywork manufactured from 1957-59, after which the factory was purchased in order to handle imported Lambettas. This Fulham Borough Council tipper was on the 1956 Commercial Motor Show stand and shows a revised, more modern-looking cab with the Perkins badge prominent. These trucks were called Trojan Seniors, not to be confused with the pre-war Senior vans. They were basically the same as the earlier vans, except they had independent front suspension and a one-piece GRP bonnet and grille. They were made for just a short time, from 1958/9, after which there was a switch to forward control vans, though there was quite a bit of overlap in production. *CHC aar108*

Right: A 25-cwt forward control van was launched at the 1958 Commercial Motor Show. Trojan also offered a passenger-carrier version. *CHC aas614*

Below: The 25-cwt forward control chassis/van/minibus was introduced for 1959 and offered until 1961. This style of van has what appears to be an aluminium body, built by another company on a Trojan chassis. It was new in late 1958 and was in service with Brazil's sausages and pies of Amersham (Bucks), Winchester (Hants) and Witney (Oxon). *CHC abb104*

UNIPOWER

1934-95

Universal Power Drives was founded in 1934 with a factory in Perivale, Middlesex and a head office in London. During the 1930s, the Unipower conversion was offered for various companies' chassis, including Fordson, Bedford, Commer and Kew Dodge. The Ford-Unipower 6x4 tractor was first trialled in 1933, while the Unipower tandem bogie used a rear relay case above the two axles.

In the 1940s and '50s, Unipower specialised in 4x4 forestry-logging trucks (Forester and then Hannibal), as well as conversions to multi-drive from 4x2 for Commer, Dodge and possibly other chassis. The company then became Unipower Ltd by 1971.

In 1972, the company launched the 4x4 Unipower Invader for firefighting and construction use. In 1977, Unipower was acquired by AC Cars Ltd and production moved to Thames Ditton, Surrey. Subsequently, the company became Unipower Vehicles Ltd.

In 1988, the company started a new business in Watford, Hertfordshire to provide continuity of support for Scammell trucks following the closure of the Rover Group (formerly British Leyland)-owned Scammell plant that year. The S24 range was introduced in 1981 by Scammell, its design based on the military and civilian uses of earlier Contractor models.

In May 1988, Unipower Vehicles Ltd acquired the design, manufacturing and support rights for the Scammell S24 range, the rear-engined crash tenders,

Commander, Contractor, Explorer, Super Constructor, Crusader, LDSS, Nubian Major and Thornycroft Antar models. Only three Unipower C series trucks were ever built: two heavy haulage and an lwb version, which used a Volvo-based normal control cab.

Alvis plc acquired the company in 1994 and named its new subsidiary Alvis Unipower Ltd, with the trucks branded as 'Alvis-Unipower'. Alvis was then acquired by BAE.

In 1992, Unipower launched its M Series chassis. (From 1994 it was marketed as Alvis-Unipower.) The series M had 8x8 drive and was designed to carry heavy loads weighing up to 24 tons or special military equipment for installation. The chassis was equipped with a 10.8-litre six-cylinder Cummins M-405E or 12/17-litre Perkins-410Tx engine. Later, the modified MH series was introduced, including two heavy truck tractors with 6x6 and 8x8 axle configurations and a gross combination weight of 110 and 117 tonnes respectively. The three-axle MH-6660 model had a 19-litre six-cylinder Cummins KTA-19-600. The four-axle MH-8875 model was equipped with the Cummins QSK-19-750 engine. Both lorries had an automatic five-speed ZF gearbox with a two-speed ZF transfer gearbox.

After being eliminated from the bidding process of the Ministry of Defence's Heavy Equipment Transporter (HET) project with the M-type tank transporter, Alvis announced its intention to seek a new owner for Alvis Unipower in autumn 1999 – seemingly without success.

Left: This photograph, taken outside the Universal Power Drives factory in Perivale, Middlesex in July 1953, shows two Unipower Forester timber tractors with Newport, Monmouthshire registrations, dating apparently from early 1950. Heavy haulage contractor Wynn's also had a timber extraction operation based in Welshpool, to which the Foresters were assigned.
Ian Allan Library

Right: After the war, Unipower offered multidrive conversions on the 'Parrot-nose' Kew Dodge 100 series chassis. This chassis-cab is noteworthy as being lhd and having six-wheel drive. It is seen here being tested by *Commercial Motor* magazine on a military testing site circa 1950. Kew Dodge chassis were exported widely, including the badged De Soto and Fargo variations. *CHC aax241*

Below: This swb Kew Dodge had a Unipower 4x4 conversion, seen here on trial with test weights by *Commercial Motor* on a military-vehicle test site in June 1951. *CHC 03004*

Left: Unipower conversions were offered on the rival Commer chassis. This March 1958 photograph shows a 6x2 extended-chassis Commer QX rated at 10 tons. From 1965, Rootes offered a factory-trailing axle or tandem-drive six-wheeler, though the Commer CA-CE chassis would be converted by Unipower. The relaunched 500K Series also had a Dodge-Unipower option, powered by the Perkins V8 540 engine. *Chas K. Bowers*

Below: The 8x8 Alvis-Unipower M8875 tractors were acquired by GCE-Alstom. One was then rebuilt and acquired by ALE for abnormal load haulage. *Len Jefferies*

VOLVO

1975-2000

AB Volvo started manufacturing cars in Hisingen, Gothenburg in 1927, with the first trucks coming off the line the following year. In November 1966, Ailsa Trucks Ltd of Barrhead, Glasgow was appointed British Volvo truck concessionaire and initially imported the forward control 4x2 F86, joined in the autumn of 1967 by the heavier 4x2 F88 and 6x2 FB88.

In 1972, Volvo acquired 75% of Ailsa Trucks, as well as an old Ministry of Defence site in Irvine, North Ayrshire. Production of modified F86 tractor units, plus 6x4S and 8x4S – the 'S' standing for 'Scottish' – started at Barrhead, then moved to Irvine in 1973. In 1975, Irvine started assembly of new 8x4 F86 models (F86-44 to -64) using Volvo components. By 1977, the new 6x4 F86 was being assembled, intended for tipper use. Some of the production even had to be exported back to Sweden.

The 1,000th vehicle to be built in Irvine was driven off the line in September 1977, by which time Irvine was also assembling all F86 tractor units for the UK, which had previously been imported. The F86 was replaced in mid-1978 by the forward control F7 with a version of the 'Club of Four' cab, used by Saviem, DAF, Magirus and Volvo. Knocked-down 4x2 rigid and tractor versions were assembled at Irvine, with three and four-axle versions also built using shipped-in components for 6x2, 6x4, 8x2 and 8x4 drive, plus a different 8x4 for Australia.

Both the F86 and F7 used variations of Volvo's TD70 6.7-litre engine, available in normally aspirated and turbocharged versions (the latter also had an intercooler option on the turbo engine). In October 1978, the company became Volvo Trucks (Great Britain) Ltd. The first Irvine-built F10 tractors were also being assembled around this time, which continued with the revised engines that were fitted from autumn 1981 onwards.

In 1979, Irvine produced an F7 'Chinese Six' 6x4 tractor with twin-steer front axles. The November 1979 Scottish Show saw the debut of the F616 16-tonne rigid, designed specifically for the British market, with a six-litre TD60 engine. In 1983, with the revised Construction & Use Regulations allowing artics up to 38 tons, Irvine added a second steering axle to the 4x2 F7, on the line if required. A 6x2 version of the F6 was also designed for refuse collection with an additional steering rear axle.

From 1980, Irvine produced a narrower series of two, three and four-axle trucks for Switzerland, which were

Right: The Irvine plant opened in May 1975, the year Ailsa Trucks Ltd became a 100% subsidiary of AB Volvo. Production lines were laid down to assemble three and four-axle F86 chassis. In June 1975, the new 8x4 chassis were announced, which replaced the 1972 type 8x4S model for the British market. The new lorry was available with five wheelbase options from 4.4-6.4 metres (14ft 5in-21ft). The designations were F86-44 to 64: smallest was the F86-44, limited to 28.5 tonnes/28 tons to conform to current Construction & Use Regulations; the other four grossed the full 30 tons gvw. Both the front axles were the same as the 4x2 F86 and the rear axles were identical to the heavier F88/89. This October 1976 photograph is of an 8x4 tipper in service with R. Hanson & Son Ltd of Wakefield, Yorkshire.

Ian Allan Library

launched at the Geneva Show: the F12-based 2.3 metre-wide CH230, with a modified F7-based sleeper cab with narrow wings. 779 were built until 1986.

In 1985, new light and medium models were introduced: the FL6 went up to 16.5 tonnes; in 1986, a new 6.7-litre-engined FL7 and 9.6-litre FL10 series replaced the F7 and F10. Irvine produced three and four-axled 6x2, 6x4 and 8x4 FL7 and twin-steer FL10 trucks. The FL6 was then offered for the fire engine market and the FL616 for the brewery market, with a stepped-down frame. By 1987, Irvine was building all versions of the FL7 and FL10 for the UK and Irish markets. Expansion meant retooling for the reintroduction of the F10 and 12-litre F12 models, which were built until 1992. The next year, a military 4x4 modified FL6, the Highlander, sold in 68 units to the Swedish Air Force.

In spring 1993, the new FH12 (with 12-litre engine) and FH16 (16-litre) were introduced. FH12 production started at Irvine in June 1995 and FL12 in August, using the FH12 engine. The FL12 was available as a two or three-axle tractor or three or four-axle rigid. In 1995, lhd FL7 and FL10 models were exported to Germany, France and the Netherlands. In 1998, the MOD ordered 121 self-loading 6x6 dump trucks based on the FL12 tipper; through the parent company, Israel also ordered 55 FH16-based 6x6 tank transporters.

In summer 1998, bus assembly was about to be switched to Poland or Sweden just as the FM replacements for the FL10/12 were about to start production. The FM7/10 and 12 replaced the FL7/19 and 12 respectively, with a new cab based on the FH version. The FM7 had a new 7.3-litre engine and the FM10, scheduled to follow

early in 1999, a new 12-litre. The FH12 received a new engine and substantial improvements.

However, with a downturn in the economy it was decided, in early 1999, to close the plant. Bus assembly was ultimately switched to Poland and Sweden, and the plant finished its last truck in 2000. Approximately 49,000 trucks had been built in total.

Above: Irvine's Modified Vehicle Assembly (MVA) department was able to build chassis to particular specifications. Volvo asked it to design and build what became the CH230 ('CH' was the country code for Switzerland and '230' the maximum width in centimeters). They used an imported F12 chassis with narrower axles, with the F7's lighter but modified sleeper cab and narrow wings. The F12's 12-litre TD120C engine required the cab to be mounted considerably higher on the F12 chassis, which in turn required additional entry steps. Most (if not all) had Trilex wheels instead of the UK market's standard disc wheels. The first order at the beginning of that year was for 198 trucks (worth £6.5 million). The model continued in production until 1986, by which time 779 had been built. They were mostly two and three-axle chassis (thus at least 4x2 and 6x4 drive), though some had four axles and a double drive for special applications such as concrete mixers. *Ian Allan Library*

Right: Ailsa Trucks Ltd became Volvo (Great Britain) Ltd in October 1978. By then Irvine were building 4x2 rigids sent 'CKD' from Sweden ('completely knocked down', i.e. kits of parts), and three and four-axle (6x2, 6x4, 8x2 and 8x4) versions of the 7-litre F7, with many components delivered by suppliers directly to the factor. Model designations F6, F7, F10 and F12 were adopted from the engine capacity (6, 7, 10 or 12 litres respectively), and then the design weight of chassis without trailer but laden. This F731 tipper had an 8x4 drive and a 16.5 cu m Neville Charrold Ultralight body. The 8x4 had either the R62 or SR62 splitter gearbox from the F10, with either the TD709G engine or, as here, the TD70F turbocharged engine. They were rated at 30 tonnes gvw and 32 or 36 tons gcw/gtw respectively. *Ian Allan Library*

Left: In November 1979, the Irvine-assembled version of the 6-litre TD60B-engined F6 series was announced. There were five wheelbase variations: 3.5m (11.5ft), 4m (13.12ft), 4.5m (14.8ft), 5m (16.4ft) and 5.5m (18ft). However, only the 3.5, 4.5 and 5.5m-wheelbase chassis were to be imported, though the other chassis could be specially ordered. The F616 rigid seen here was in service with Ellerpack (Warehousing) Ltd of Rotherham, South Yorkshire. *Ian Allan Library*

Left: The three-axle F7 series was available as a 6x2 or 6x4, with the TD 70G naturally aspirated engine and eight-speed R52 gearbox. The ratings were 24 tonnes gvw and 32 tons gcw/gtw. This 1980 F727 was in service with Central Farmers Ltd of Leven, Fife, and had a bulk-flow body. *Ian Allan Library*

Right: The F7 4x2 rigid options were either powered by the TD 70G or TD 70F turbo engines with the R52 gearbox. They ran at either 16 tonnes or 16.5 tons gvw and either 32 tonnes or 36 tons gcw/ gtw respectively. This 1980 F717 had the sleeper cab option and was new to Newton Haulage Ltd of Harlington, Bedfordshire. *Ian Allan Library*

Right: The new light and medium model FL6 range (Forward control and Low entry with light cab) was introduced in 1985, with weights up to 16,500kg and the 5.44-litre 209bhp engine. In the spring of 1989, changes at the lighter end of the Volvo range meant that the FL608/609/610/611 were plated at 7.5-11 tonnes, with the 5.44 litre TD61G 152bhp engine and Eaton six-speed gearbox. This 1989/90 FL617 refrigerated van was presumably plated at 16.5 tonnes, and it was operated by Herbert Fletcher Transport Ltd of Hull, East Yorkshire. *PM Photography*

Right: In 1987, Irvine was building all versions of the FL7 and FL10 that had been introduced the previous year. Capacity was to be increased and new tooling installed to accommodate the reintroduction of the F10 and F12 models. This F10 tractor had an intercooled version of the 9.6-litre engine that produced 299bhp. It had been introduced along with the non-intercooled version a few years previously, as well as a new day cab with a higher windscreen than the previous short version. This outfit was in service with the London Rubber Co. *PM Photography*

Left: In the summer of 1991, the FS7 was launched. This new model was essentially an FL6 with the more-powerful intercooled and turbocharged TD73E low-emission 6.7-litre engine for operation as an articulated or draw-bar tractor at up to 32.5 tonnes, and also for fire appliances. This 1993/4-registered FS7 17 was coupled to a milk tanker trailer in service with Milk Marque, the successor to the Milk Marketing Board. *PM Photography*

Below: Spring 1993 saw the replacement of the F12 and 16-litre F16 by the new FH12/FH16 with new cabs: 'Forward control High cab'. The FH12 had a new 12-litre engine and options of day, sleeper and more-luxurious Globetrotter cabs (intended for continental trips). The first Irvine-built FH was launched on 1 June 1995. This 1995-6 FH12 was operated by Cotteswold Dairy Ltd of Tewkesbury, Gloucestershire. *PM Photography*

Right: In the summer of 1998, the Gothenburg and Irvine plants started simultaneous assembly of the new FM series – FM7, FM10 and FM12 – that replaced the FL range. The FM range cab was based on the FH but mounted lower. This 1999 FM7 had the new 7.3-litre D7C engine that replaced the 6.7-litre, and 290bhp as against the 250bhp version. *PM Photography*

Below: Production at Irvine ended in week 17 of 2000, which most likely equates to April of that year. This FM7 six-wheeler was new in 1999/2000 and must have been assembled just before the end. It was in service with Nicholas Rowell Haulage, based at Torrs Quarry (East Alklington, Totnes) just outside Kingsbridge, Devon. *PM Photography*

VULCAN

1903-53

The Vulcan Motor and Engineering Co of Southport, Lancashire made cars from 1902-28 and commercial vehicles until 1931, when the company went into receivership. However, the receiver managed to keep production going until 1937, when what remained of the company was taken over by Tilling-Stevens of Maidstone, Kent. In fact, the company was sold to trailer manufacturer J. Brockhouse, which only wanted the works and the land, production being moved to Tilling-Stevens' Maidstone works.

Some 'Vulcans' were produced for essential users during World War 2, but production restarted in earnest afterwards. However, no sooner had the range been reestablished than Tilling-Stevens was in turn taken over by the Rootes Group in 1950, with a new 7-ton artic appearing at that year's Commercial Motor Show in London. Rootes had its own established commercial vehicle makers in Commer and Karrier and both Vulcan and Tilling-Stevens vanished finally in 1953, although the Commer TS3 two-stroke diesel was inherited from Tilling-Stevens. At that time, the range included a forward control six-tonner fitted with a Perkins P6 diesel engine.

Left: Vulcan Motors Ltd of Maidstone, Kent continued to supply lorries to the civilian market during World War 2, and then continued post-war. This shot is dated December 1945 and shows chassis No 6 (VF 1402), which was supplied by Hampshire distributor the Vickers Motor Body Co Ltd to T. Oakley, horse and cattle transporter of New Milton. The body was by J. H. Jennings & Son of Sandbach, Cheshire. *Ian Allan Library*

Left: This shot is dated September 1945 and shows a wartime five-tonner with the mid-war modifications, including improved visibility from the enlarged windscreen panels. It was in service with J. Goodacre & Sons, haulage contractor of Hathern, Leicestershire, and was photographed outside the likely supplying dealer, Ford & Slater of Leicester, which was also Perkins' agent. Note the service van in front. *Ian Allan Library*

Above: This 1948-registered Perkins-engined 7GF swb 7-ton tractor was photographed in the mid-1950s. It was in service with Eltham Transport Co Ltd of south London and used to carry earth-moving equipment for building projects. *CHC aay385*

Left: Photographed in Louth, Lincolnshire, this 1952-registered 5-ton flatbed rigid was operated by Theodore West & Co Ltd. By the time the photograph was taken, Vulcans may have ceased production. *CHC aak408*

Right: Vulcans were exported with both rhd and lhd, the latter seen here on this 7GF lwb seven-tonner at the 1948 London Commercial Motor Show. It was destined for Danish Dairies in Copenhagen. *CHC aau300*

Below: This photo was taken in the West Country. The Vulcan on the left was new in 1948 and had a Perkins engine. The operator was a member of the Road Haulage Association, shown by the badges on the Vulcan and the adjacent Perkins-engined wartime Seddon. *CHCabc310*